THE HÁVAMÁL

THE HÁVAMÁL

WITH SELECTIONS FROM OTHER POEMS OF THE EDDA, ILLUSTRATING THE WISDOM OF THE NORTH IN HEATHEN TIMES

EDITED AND TRANSLATED BY

D. E. MARTIN CLARKE

SOMETIME MARION KENNEDY STUDENT
OF NEWNHAM COLLEGE, CAMBRIDGE.

CAMBRIDGE
AT THE UNIVERSITY PRESS
1923

CAMBRIDGE UNIVERSITY PRESS
Cambridge, New York, Melbourne, Madrid, Cape Town,
Singapore, São Paulo, Delhi, Tokyo, Mexico City

Cambridge University Press
The Edinburgh Building, Cambridge CB2 8RU, UK

Published in the United States of America by Cambridge University Press, New York

www.cambridge.org
Information on this title: www.cambridge.org/9781107679764

First published 1923
First paperback edition 2011

A catalogue record for this publication is available from the British Library

ISBN 978-1-107-67976-4 Paperback

PREFACE

THE Hávamál is of unique interest as being the only work in Norse, or any other Teutonic Language, which embodies the philosophy of heathen times. Up to now it has not been easily accessible to English readers. It has been published only in editions of the Edda poems or still larger collections, and with the exception of one edition which contains a line by line translation but very few notes, these have all been out of print for many years. In addition to the poem itself the present edition contains extracts from three other poems (including the greater part of the Sigrdrífumál), which serve to illustrate the maxims or the magic of the Hávamál.

The editor's thanks are due to the Syndics of the University Press for undertaking the publication of the book, and to the staff for the efficient manner in which the corrections have been carried out; to Newnham College for the award of the Marion Kennedy Studentship and to the Trustees of the Earl of Moray Fund for generous grants, which together have enabled her to bring it to completion; and to Professor and Mrs Chadwick for assistance in the preparation and revision of the work.

7 *November* 1922.

TABLE OF CONTENTS

ABBREVIATIONS

Aarb∮*ger*—*Aarb*∮*ger for nordisk Oldkyndighed og Historie*, Copenhagen, 1866- .

Arkiv—*Arkiv för nordisk Filologi*, Christiania, 1883-8 ; Lund, 1889- .

Bugge—*Studier over de nordiske Gude- og Heltesagns Oprindelse*, Christiania, 1881- .

C. P. B.—*Corpus Poeticum Boreale*, G. Vigfusson and F. York Powell, Oxford, 1883.

Du Chaillu—*The Viking Age*, London, 1889.

Detter and Heinzel—*Sæmundar Edda*, Leipzig, 1903.

Egilsson—*Lexicon Poeticum Antiquae Linguae Septentrionalis*, revised and translated into Danish by F. Jónsson, Copenhagen, 1916.

Fritzner—*Ordbog over det gamle norske Sprog*, Christiania, 1886-96.

F. Jónsson—*Den Oldnorske og Oldislandske Litteraturs Historie*, Copenhagen, 1894.

Grimm—*Deutsche Mythologie*, translated by Stallybrass, London, 1888.

Hammershaimb—*Fær*∮*sk Anthologi*, Copenhagen, 1891.

Mogk—*Geschichte der Norwegisch-Isländischen Literatur*, Strassburg, 1904.

Noreen—*Altisländische und Altnorwegische Grammatik*, Halle, 1903.

Saxo—Saxo Grammaticus, *Gesta Danorum*, ed. Holder, Strassburg, 1886. In Books I—IX the references are usually to the pages of O. Elton's translation, London, 1894.

Vigfusson—*An Icelandic-English Dictionary*, by R. Cleasby and G. Vigfusson, Oxford, 1874.

In the *Íslendinga Sögur* (*Isl. Sög.*) and the *Fornaldar Sögur* (*F. A. S.*) the references are to the editions published by S. Kristjánsson, Reykjavík.

INTRODUCTION

I. THE POETRY OF THE EDDA

In the early literature of the Teutonic peoples, as in that of the Greeks and many other nations, didactic poetry plays an important part. In English it is prominent from the time of our earliest records. We may refer for example to the series of sententious utterances varying from definitions to maxims which are usually known as gnomic poems, and to many other pieces, the object of which is to classify knowledge derived from various phases of human experience or to impart information of a moral or religious character. Even narrative poetry, and in particular the epic *Beowulf*, contains a not inconsiderable amount of gnomic and other didactic material.

In Norse poetry earlier than 1150[1] the didactic element is for the most part confined to the large group of anonymous poems collectively known as the *Edda*, or—more fully—*Sæmundar Edda* or the "Older Edda." It is unnecessary here to discuss the suitability of these names, which are due to surmises made by scholars of the seventeenth century. They are at all events convenient as a means of distinguishing the poems in question from the poetry usually known as Skaldic, which is for the most part the work of known authors. Unlike the latter, which deals mainly—though by no means exclusively—with contemporaneous events, the "Edda" poems are concerned only with persons known from legend alone, with the gods, and with human beings collectively. It is customary to divide the group into two classes—those which deal with characters whose stories are derived from heroic tradition, and those which are concerned with the divine, the general, and

---

[1] The poem *Málsháttakvæði* is generally believed to date from a later period. It is attributed by Möbius to Bjarni Kolbeinsson, Bishop of Orkney, 1188–1282.

characters of folk tale. The didactic element is to be found
for the most part in the latter class. There is however one
important exception—a group of three poems usually regarded as forming a connected trilogy—in which, though
the characters are heroic, the didactic element is prominent
(cf. pp. 15 f.). Moreover, in this case the treatment of the
story is in conformity with that of folk tale rather than with
that of heroic poetry.

The non-heroic poems of the Edda show in general a
strong resemblance to certain early Greek poetic works—
in some cases to the poems of Hesiod, in others to the
Homeric Hymns. With the latter we may compare the
narrative mythological poems *Þrymskviða* and *Hymiskviða*.
As for Hesiod, we have an analogy on the one hand between
the *Theogony* and *Völuspá*, on the other between the *Works
and Days* and the *Hávamál*. While the two former deal
almost exclusively with mythological information, in the two
latter this element is subordinate, and the bulk of both poems
is occupied with instruction of a practical character, some of
which might be classed as ethical, using the word in the
widest sense. The chief difference between the Greek and
Norse poems is the prominence given in the latter to magic.
Apart from incidental references, the *Hávamál* contains a
whole series of strophes which may be described as a spell
song, and there are similar passages in the *Sigrdrífumál* and
the *Grógaldr*. It is with these two elements in the poems,
practical instruction and magical wisdom, that we are mainly
concerned here.

The metrical form of the Edda poems, as indeed of all
early Norse poetry, differs from that of Anglo-Saxon and of
the earliest German verse in being strophic. The complicated
metres found in the Skaldic poems do not occur in the Edda.
The metres most usually employed in the latter are those
generally known as *fornyrðislag* and *lióðaháttr*, in both of
which the strophe normally consists of four lines[1]. In the
former these lines are all of similar form and represent what

---

[1] For variations of the normal *fornyrðislag* strophe, cp. Sievers, *Altgerm.
Metrik*, § 42.

is commonly known as the "Teutonic alliterative verse." The line is divided by a caesura into two parts—each of which is regarded as containing two accented syllables, of which either one or both in the first half-line and one (usually the first) in the second half-line must alliterate[1].

In the *lióðaháttr* metre the lines are of unequal length, alternately long and short. In its relationship to the *fornyrðislag* this metre bears at least a superficial resemblance to the classical elegiac as compared with consecutive hexameter verse, and, as in the Latin elegiac, there is usually a break at the end of each short line. The long lines are of similar structure to those of the *fornyrðislag*, though greater freedom is allowed. The short line usually contains three accented syllables, of which any two (rarely all three) alliterate. The alliteration[2] is independent of that of the preceding or following line and there is no caesura. The *lióðaháttr* strophe, like that of the *fornyrðislag*, usually contains four lines. We find however strophes of five lines in which either the first or the second long line is followed by two short lines[3], and less frequently strophes of six lines which contain two pairs of short lines. Occasionally we meet with three short lines[4] in succession, and with long strophes containing as many as three long and six short lines. The strophe however always begins with a long line, and it may be observed that where two or three short lines occur in succession the second and third usually repeat or supplement the idea contained in the first. Snorri in his *Háttatal*[5] gives the name *galdralag* to a five-line strophe ending with two short lines, but it is not certain that the term was restricted to this particular variety.

The *fornyrðislag*, like the Greek hexameter, is generally used in narrative poems. In the heroic poems it is indeed almost universal, but in those dealing with stories of the gods

---

[1] In connection with the *fornyrðislag* we may mention also the *málaháttr* which is regarded by many as merely a variety of it. The difference lies in the fact that whereas the normal *fornyrðislag* half-line consists of four units, two accented and two unaccented, the normal *málaháttr* half-line contains an additional unit, five units in all.

[2] Cp. Phillpotts, *Elder Edda*, p. 92.

[3] E.g. str. 1, 105.   [4] E.g. str. 125.

[5] Str. 101.

it is as a rule limited to pieces of a more or less narrative character, e.g. *þrymskviða* and *Völuspá.*

The wisdom poetry with which we are concerned here is almost wholly in the *lióðaháttr* metre. The trilogy (*Reginsmál, Fáfnismál* and *Sigrdrífumál*) contains a certain number of strophes in *fornyrðislag*, and in the main, as in the *Hákonarmál*, these verses deal with narrative while the rest, by far the greater number, are in *lióðaháttr*. Even the *Hávamál* itself contains a certain number of *fornyrðislag* strophes[1]. For the most part these consist of catalogues, and the choice of the *fornyrðislag* in such cases may be partly due to the fact that it is capable of containing a larger number of names or terms.

[1] 81–83, 85–87, 89–90, 144, and perhaps parts of other strophes, e.g. 137 and 145. In most of these strophes, however, the metre is very irregular—a combination of *fornyrðislag* with *málaháttr* (see p. 3, note 1), the latter predominating.

II. THE HÁVAMÁL

1. THE TEXT

The text of the *Hávamál* occupies just over four-and-a-half folios of the Codex Regius (No. 2365 R.), a vellum dating from the thirteenth[1] century, and one of a collection presented to the crown of Denmark in 1662. It is still preserved in the Royal Library, Copenhagen. The poem, with the title *Hávamál*, follows the *Völuspá* in the MS, and is in good condition and with but little difficulty is decipherable throughout[2]. It is on this MS that the text of the following edition is based. Apart from this the poem is also preserved in a number of paper MSS dating from the latter part of the seventeenth and from the eighteenth centuries. Some of these contain readings divergent from those of the vellum, and also certain passages which are not found in it[3].

Although the earliest MS only dates from the thirteenth century, certain references in early literature seem to point to parts of the poem being known at an earlier date. Str. 76[1] and 77[1] occur in the last strophe of the *Hákonarmál*—a poem celebrating the death of Haakon the Good at the battle of Fitje 960, by Eyvindr Skaldaspillir. In *Fjölsvinnsmál* 20 a very probable reference is to be found to str. 138 of the *Hávamál* in the expression *af hverjum rótum rennr*, though the date of this poem is disputed[4]. Lastly, in *Fóstbrœðra Saga* VII, in a story which relates to the year 1025, we find what seems to be a quotation from str. 84 of the *Hávamál*.

[1] Middle of the thirteenth century, Mogk: latter half of the thirteenth century, F. Jónsson.

[2] I have used the photographed copy: *Codex regius af den ældre Edda i fototypisk og diplomatisk gengivelse, udgivet ved* L. F. A. Wimmer *og* F. Jónsson, Copenhagen, 1891.

[3] Bugge, *Sæmundar-Edda*, p. lvii.

[4] Only paper MSS of this poem are preserved. Mogk and F. Jónsson attribute it to the tenth century but Falk and Heusler to the thirteenth century.

More certain references are to be found in the works of Snorri. Str. 1 is quoted in the *Gylfaginning* II, and a knowledge of str. 144 ff. seems to be shown in *Bragarœður* and in *Ynglinga Saga* VI and VII. These references however do not carry us more than half a century further back than the date of the Codex Regius itself.

2. COMPONENT ELEMENTS OF THE POEM

Although the *Hávamál* is clearly a composite work containing very diverse elements, in its present form it is preserved as one poem with a single title and with all its wisdom ascribed to one person—the god Óðinn[1]. The part he plays in such poems as the *Vafðrúðnismál* and the *Grímnismál*, and his reputation as the wisest of the Aesir, make him specially suited to his rôle in the *Hávamál*.

Müllenhoff[2] was the first editor to call attention to the composite character of the poem. According to him it consists of elements which were originally independent, and with him substantially F. Jónsson would seem to agree. The latter divides the poem in the following way:

I. 1–83, gnomic; II. 84–102, the incident of *Billingr's* daughter; III. 104–110, the incident of *Gunnlöð*; IV. 111–137, the *Loddfáfnismál*; V. 138–145, the *Rúnatals þáttr*; VI. 146–163, the *Lióðatal*; VII. 164, the concluding strophe.

An examination of the Codex Regius MS seems to indicate that in two places at least the scribe meant to suggest new sections of the poem. The initial letters in both str. 111 and 138 are larger than any ordinary capital letter, and the first word of the latter strophe begins a new line in the MS. These indications would however be of little value were it not that in both cases there is an unmistakable change in theme—in the former case marked also by the use of a

---

[1] The literary device of ascribing to gods or famous kings commandments and general wise advice is not uncommon. We may compare the instructions of Ahura Mazda to Zarathustra in the Zend-Avesta, most of the Hebrew Proverbs of Solomon, the Wisdom of Cormac MacAirt and the Proverbs of Alfred.

[2] Müllenhoff, *Deutsche Alterthumskunde*, 1883, v. pp. 250–279. According to him the poem may be divided as follows. I. 1–78, 80; II A. 79, 81–102; II B. 103–110; IV. 111–137, 164; V. 138–145; VI. 146–163.

regular formula in the strophes. The other suggested divisions of the poem are not so obvious, though there is a clear break in sense after str. 146, where the spell song begins. The first hundred and ten strophes of the *Hávamál* have so much unity of spirit and style that one is inclined to infer that they must originally have been one poem[1]. The incidents in the latter part illustrate the maxims in the earlier part, and I cannot myself see any cogent reason for denying that they may have been composed originally for this purpose. At all events they have been so carefully chosen and so welded together that scholars cannot come to an agreement about the line of division. From the nature however of the subject-matter of str. 1-95 it is clear that individual strophes may have been inserted at different times, even if one does not entirely agree with F. Jónsson's suggestions. He considers the following to be later accretions: str. 8, 9, 15, 16, 18, 22, 28, 38, 42, 46, 48, 49, 63, 73-75, 78-83, 85-90, 92, 94[2].

There can be no doubt that a break occurs at str. 110. The rest of the poem from str. 110 to the end is as we have seen generally regarded as consisting of three different elements—the *Loddfáfnismál*, the *Rúnatals þáttr* and the *Lióðatal*. The *Loddfáfnismál* consists of twenty-six strophes, which, with six exceptions, are all addressed to Loddfáfnir and characterised by the formula *ráðomk þér* etc. The *Rúnatals þáttr*, str. 138–145, is devoid of such literary devices. Most of its subject-matter is very obscure. This may be due to the fact that so little is known about the myth referred to, or to the loss of strophes, or to the welding together of different fragments. The *Lióðatal* consists of eighteen spell songs each beginning with the phrase *þat kann ek*.

From the point of view of style the bulk of these strophes, from 111 to the end, show as much unity as the first hundred and ten strophes. As indicated above the majority are characterised by conventional formulae. Str. 111 seems to be

---

[1] Mogk, *Geschichte der Norwegisch-Isländischen Literatur*, Strassburg, 1904, p. 587.

[2] These strophes are printed in small type in his edition of the *Sæmundar-Edda*, Reykjavík, 1905.

intended as an introduction[1]; str. 164 is a conventional conclusion. Moreover the facts that str. 112–137 are addressed to Loddfáfnir, whose name recurs in str. 162, and that str. 164 is reminiscent of str. 111, certainly would suggest that at any rate str. 112–137 and str. 146–163 belonged originally to one poem. Those scholars therefore who wish to separate the spell song from the *Loddfáfnismál* are obliged to transfer these strophes or regard them as later additions.

The introductory strophe 111 needs some consideration, as its interpretation seems to depend on its punctuation. Gering's suggestion is perhaps the simplest—a colon after *þular stóli á*, in which case the phrase *Urðar brunni at* would be linked in meaning with the third line of the strophe. In the *Völuspá* 22 we learn that the *Urðar brunnr* (the Spring of Fate) was situated beneath the ash Yggdrasill, and Snorri in the *Gylfaginning* xv tells us that it was here that the gods held their tribunal[2]. It would seem then as if str. 111 introduces information overheard at a meeting of the gods—a parallel for which is to be found in the Life of St Ansgar[3]. It must however be noted here that the punctuation adopted above is not in accordance with the general structure of the *lióða-háttr* strophe. Normally, although the short line is alliteratively independent of the preceding long line, syntactically it is dependent on it, and in the majority of cases the break in the thought of a *lióðaháttr* strophe occurs at the end of the short line. There are however a few exceptions to this general rule—e.g. in *Hávamál* 69, where the break occurs after the first long line, and in *Grímnismál* 29, 30, where the sense runs on to the following long lines.

We may however punctuate with Neckel—a semi-colon after *Urðar brunni at*—and the strophe would then seem capable of two interpretations. Firstly the speaker may be Óðinn (the

[1] Cp. Mogk (p. 588), who considers that the words *manna mál, rúnar, ráðom* refer respectively to the three sections—hence the three sections are united by str. 111.

[2] *Gylfaginning* xv. *undir þeiri rót er brunnr sá er mjök er heilagr er heitir Urðarbrunnr; þar eigu goðin dómstað sinn....*

[3] Rembertus, *Vita S. Anscharii*, xxiii. During the second mission of St Ansgar to Sweden, a man came to King Óláfr at Birca and stated that he had been present at an assembly of the gods, who had sent him to deliver a message to the king and nation.

fimbul-þulr) speaking in his own person at the Spring of Fate either under an assumed name Loddfáfnir or to a person called Loddfáfnir, according as one interprets the relationship of *svá* to the following strophes. The meaning of the latter part of the strophe however hardly fits either of these suggestions. Or secondly the expression *Urðar brunni* at may be a reference to a heathen sanctuary like the famous one at Upsala described by Adam of Bremen in his History of the Church of Hamburg. If the claim made by the *þulr* is that his wisdom was acquired from such a sanctuary, we may compare this passage with the description of the giving of the laws to the Old Prussians[1]. One objection to this suggestion lies in the fact that *Urðar brunnr* is only known to us as an abstract conception associated with the world-tree. Like other elements in the conception of Yggdrasill's Ash it may have had earthly prototypes, but we have no evidence that any sacred springs were known as Springs of Fate.

Of these three possible interpretations the one regarding the speaker as Óðinn seems the least probable, even apart from the fact that it does not fit in well with the last part of the strophe. It is unnatural to interpret the words *segja svá* other than as indicating that what follows is a direct report of the speech heard[2]. We may therefore place the following verses in inverted commas. If the person who heard the speech is not Loddfáfnir, then his name must be placed outside the inverted commas in each case—which is not probable.

Again the identity of the person speaking to Loddfáfnir in str. 112–137 is not disclosed. From str. 138–146 the speaker is Óðinn addressing a nameless *þú*. From str. 147 the speaker is almost certainly Óðinn addressing Loddfáfnir (cp. str. 162). If we are right in believing that these three sets of strophes are parts of one original poem, we must conclude that Loddfáfnir is the person addressed in the second

---

[1] Grunau, *Preussische Chronik*, ed. M. Perlbach, Leipzig, 1876–7, Tract. III. cap. I. 2.

[2] Cp. an interesting parallel in Proverbs xxxi, where gnomic verses are introduced in the following way: "The words of king Lemuel, the prophecy that his mother taught him... 'It is not for kings, O Lemuel, it is not for kings to drink wine etc.'"

as well as in the first and third series, and that Óðinn is the speaker (as reported by Loddfáfnir) in the first as well as in the second and third series. In that case Loddfáfnir cannot be identical with Óðinn.

The most reasonable conclusion then seems to be that in str. 111 Loddfáfnir[1] is the person who is about to chant (þylja) and that it is from Óðinn that he has received his instructions— whatever be the punctuation we may adopt in line 2. The phrases *manna mál* and *þögðo* can hardly be considered a valid objection against this interpretation, since the use of the plural for the singular is extremely common in Norse, as in Anglo-Saxon poetry. It may however be that the plural is used because a number of divine beings are regarded as being present, though Óðinn is the actual speaker.

The word *þulr* which occurs in this strophe is used in three other places in the *Hávamál*—in str. 134 in its simple form, in str. 80 and 142 in the compound *fimbul-þulr*. It is only found twice elsewhere in the Edda, in *Vafðrúðnismál* 9 and in *Fáfnismál* 34. With the exception probably of *Fáfnismál* 34, all these examples emphasise the wisdom of the *þulr*, and most of them his great age. The use of the word however in the *Hávamál* 111 (with its related *þylja* and *þular stóli*) points to a technical meaning which is lacking in the other examples in the Edda.

There are other indications which suggest that the meaning of the word was not at all times the same. In the use of *þylsk* (*Hávamál* 17) to describe the babbling of a fool, and in the title of *inn hára þul* given to Reginn by the birds in the *Fáfnismál*, we seem to have a debased meaning of the word[2]. It seems clear moreover that in Skaldic poetry *þulr* simply meant a poet[3], which can scarcely be true of some of

---

[1] For further suggestions as to the identity of Loddfáfnir, cp. Mogk, *Gesch. d. Norw.-Isl. Lit.* p. 588; Sijmons, *Die Lieder der Edda* 1906, *Einleitung*, pp. clxvii ff. The meaning of the word is obscure. Cp. Detter and Heinzel, II. p. 129. *Lodd-* is usually connected with *loddarar* who are classed with jesters and fiddlers in *Thiðreks Saga* cxxvi. Compare also Anglo-Saxon *loddere*, 'beggar,' and M.H.G. adjective *loter*, 'loose,' 'light,' 'frivolous.' *-fáfnir* is found in the name of the dragon Fáfnir, but the meaning is unknown.

[2] Cp. also perhaps the name of the river *Fimbul-þul*, *Grímnismál* 27.

[3] *Flateyjarbók*, II. p. 487; *Íslendinga drápa*, str. 18.

the passages in which the word occurs in the Edda. For the use of the word with yet another meaning we may turn to the Anglo-Saxon *þyle*, which is used in glossaries to translate *orator*. A man called Hunferð described as *þyle* plays an important part in the *Beowulf*. He is clearly an important member of the court, sits at the feet of his lord, the King of the Danes, is allowed to make an insolent speech to Beowulf, and finally lends him the sword called Hrunting[1].

One further example must be mentioned. On a runic stone[2] found at Snoldelev in Sjælland there is inscribed an epitaph in runes which runs thus: "The stone of Gunnvaldr, son of Hróaldr, *þulr* at Salhaugar." This is believed to belong to the ninth century.

It is generally agreed[3] that the word *þulr* originally had a religious significance, though its etymology unfortunately is obscure[4]. It may not however be out of place here to point out that some at least of its usages suggest a certain resemblance to those of the Irish word *file*, which seems originally to have meant a prophet or seer[5], perhaps the *vates* of whom we hear so frequently in ancient notices relating to the Gauls. Óðinn (the *fimbul-þulr* of the *Hávamál* 80 and 142) is described by Saxo in one passage as *Uggerus vates*, and the general description of this god in the Edda and other early Norse records is at least not incompatible with such a character. The human prototypes which gave rise to such a conception may have been persons similar to the ancient Greek prophet Teiresias or some of the prophets of the Old Testament such as Samuel or Elijah[6].

It is in the last strophe that the title of the poem—*Hávamál*—comes, and there is considerable difference of opinion as to whether it belongs properly to the whole work or only

[1] *Beowulf*, ll. 501, 1165, 1455.
[2] Wimmer, *Danske Runemindesmærker*, II. pp. 338 ff.
[3] Sijmons, *Die Lieder der Edda, Einleitung*, p. clxvii; Ólrík, *Danske Studier*, 1909, pp. 1 ff., 'At sidde på höj'; Phillpotts, *The Elder Edda*, pp. 189 ff.
[4] Fick, *Wörterbuch der Indogermanischen Grundsprache s.v.*, Göttingen, 1890, vol. III.
[5] The word *file* occurs first (in feminine form) in the name of the German prophetess *Veleda* who enjoyed such great veneration in the time of Vespasian.
[6] The picture suggested in str. 111 perhaps invites a comparison with the Delphic Oracle, though the resemblance is only partial.

to some part of it. Vigfusson and Powell held that it applies
only to the *Lióðatal,* while Müllenhoff thought that it belonged properly to the *Loddfáfnismál* and that the original
position of str. 164 was immediately after str. 137; F. Jónsson
however holds that the strophe was originally composed for
its present place as an epilogue to the whole work. As indicated above (pp. 7 f.) I see no reason for doubting the sub-
stantial unity of str. 111–164; and I suspect that it was to
this portion rather than to the whole poem as we have it
that the title *Hávamál* originally belonged.

3. The date and locality of the poem

The fact that the *Hávamál* is a composite poem makes
the problem of dating it a difficult one. Phrases in poems
of the tenth century may point to its existence at that time
(cf. p. 5), but in view of the nature of the subject-matter it
is clear that additions may have been made during a very
considerable[1] period. Undoubtedly for the greater part of
this period the poem was handed down by oral tradition.

A consideration of the poem as a whole however suggests
that the bulk of it must be ascribed to the heathen period[2].
The philosophy of the gnomic strophes is such that it could
hardly have been expressed at a time and in a country which
had accepted Christianity. Moreover the tone of the *Lodd-*
fáfnismál, with its probable allusion to a heathen sanctuary
(str. 111), is purely pagan, and above all it is difficult to
believe that the spell song could have been composed at
a later period. The same remark applies to the difficult
strophes 138 ff. in which we seem to get a glimpse of certain
mysteries of the old religion, of which even Snorri[3] tells us
nothing.

F. Jónsson dates all sections of the *Hávamál* in the first
quarter of the tenth century with the exception of the *Lodd-*
fáfnismál, which he ascribes to the last quarter of the ninth
century[4]. Müllenhoff dates no part of the poem earlier than

---

[1] Mogk, p. 587.
[2] Mogk, p. 573; F. Jónsson, i. p. 65.
[3] Cp. however, Bugge, *Studier,* i. pp. 292 ff.; Golther, *Handbuch der germ.*
Myth. pp. 350 ff.   [4] *Op. cit.* pp. 65, 66 and 239.

900. Mogk suggests that some of the *Hávamál* fragments may belong to the earliest period of Old Norse poetry—that is to the early ninth century[1].

It seems unwise in view of the nature of the evidence at one's disposal to hazard anything more than an approximate date, if the poem is to be assigned to the heathen period. One or two observations may serve to make this clear. In str. 71, 81 and perhaps also 70 there are references to cremation, which F. Jónsson and Vigfusson discount on the ground that such phrases are proverbial and offer no proof that the poem was composed when cremation was the custom. There is however no valid reason why these strophes should not date back to the early ninth century—when cremation was probably still fairly common both in Norway[2] and in Sweden—and for that matter to an even earlier period. The fact that there are at least two references to cremation and none to inhumation might even be taken as substantiating the latter suggestion.

There are moreover in the *Hávamál* a certain number of ἅπ. λεγ. and words and phrases of obscure meaning (e.g. *taugreptr, á bröndom, endreðögo, trémaðr*), while other words are used with an unusual significance (e.g. *þorp*). These perhaps point to familiarity with customs and things which had fallen into desuetude.

Modern scholars seem to have little doubt that the bulk of the *Hávamál* originated in Norway and not in Iceland[3]. This is substantiated not only by most of the local colouring, which is unmistakably Norwegian, but also by the diction. The most striking examples of the former are the references to the young fir-tree (str. 50), the bark for thatching (str. 60), and the *bautarsteinar* (str. 72)[4]. That the original home of the poem was Norway seems also to be suggested

---

[1] *Op. cit.* p. 87.
[2] For cremation in the Viking Age, cp. (for Norway) Gustafson, *Norges Oldtid*, p. 122; (for Sweden) Montelius, *Sveriges Historia*[2], i. p. 289; cp. also S. Müller, *Nord. Alt.* ii. pp. 256 ff.
[3] The question is complicated by the composite nature of the poem and the difficulty of ascertaining with certainty what are later insertions. We may refer to str. 134 which E. Magnússon maintains has Icelandic colouring.
[4] Cp. also F. Jónsson, i. 232 f.

by the occurrence in certain strophes of words not used elsewhere in Old Norse literature, but preserved as late as the
nineteenth century in the Norwegian *landsmaal*. At least
four such ἅπ. λεγ. are recorded by Aasen in his Norwegian
Dialect Dictionary—*kópa* (str. 17), *snópa* (str. 33), *glissa*
(str. 31), *glama* (str. 31). It seems likely moreover in the
case of other words that the dialectal meaning given by
Aasen is more suited to the *Hávamál* context than the
ordinary meaning attached to them in Old Norse literature.
Finally the allusions to cremation are an important factor in
localising the poem, for the sagas show that in Iceland it
was almost entirely used for laying troublesome ghosts.

III. THE SIGRDRÍFUMÁL, REGINSMÁL AND GRÓGALDR; TEXT, DATE AND LOCALITY

In the Codex Regius there are three poems which are now usually known as the *Reginsmál*, the *Fáfnismál* and the *Sigrdrífumál*[1]. They follow one another without a break and form a trilogy giving a connected story—if they are not really to be regarded as a single poem. The subject of the trilogy is the youth of the hero Sigurðr and his early adventures—the vengeance executed on the sons of Hundingr (*Reginsmál*), the slaying of the dragon Fáfnir (*Fáfnismál*), and the awakening of the valkyrie Sigrdrífa[2], together with her advice to the hero (*Sigrdrífumál*).

For a consideration of the whole of the *Reginsmál* the reader is referred to F. Jónsson, I. pp. 268 ff. and to Mogk, pp. 628 ff.

The main part of the *Reginsmál* deals first with the story told by Reginn to Sigurðr, and secondly with the omens of victory given by Óðinn disguised as Hnikarr to Sigurðr on his expedition against the sons of Hundingr. The latter are in the *lióðaháttr* metre and are conjectured by F. Jónsson to be of earlier date than the rest of the poem. These strophes are also preserved in the *Nornagests þáttr* (Cod. Arnam. nr. 62 fol.), and the *Flateyjarbók* (Cod. Regius nr. 1005 fol.), with slight differences in the text[3]. They are similar to certain gnomic strophes in the *Hávamál* and to the 'runes' in the *Sigrdrífumál* and are generally believed to have been composed in the tenth century and to have originated in Norway[4].

The *Sigrdrífumál* contains a series of spell songs and a series of gnomic strophes—both of which have been trans-

---

[1] The titles *Fáfnismál* and *Sigrdrífumál* are taken from the paper MSS; *Reginsmál* is a title given by Bugge and very generally adopted by editors.

[2] In *Fáfnismál* 44 occurs the genitive *Sigrdrífar* which would necessitate a nominative *Sigrdríf*; the weak form however occurs in paper MSS.

[3] Cp. notes where the differences are noted if MS R. is obscure.

[4] Cp. str. 21, *tái*, and the reference to wolves (str. 22).

lated and annotated below. The *Sigrdrífumál* is to be found
in its completest form in two paper MSS: Codex A.M. 738
written in 1680 (according to Bugge), and Codex A.M. 166 b,
later in the century. The best text is in the Codex Regius,
which however is cut short at str. 29 owing to the loss of
several leaves of the MS. Str. 5–21 are quoted in full in the
Völsunga Saga, where also is to be found a prose paraphrase
of the rest of the strophes of the poem. Up to. str. 29
my text is based on the Codex Regius (with references to
the *Völsunga Saga* version in the notes); after that I have
followed the paper MSS together with the *Völsunga Saga.*
There is nothing to indicate that str. 37 is the concluding
strophe of the original poem, though no further precepts are
given in *Völsunga Saga*[1].

In its extant form the *Sigrdrífumál* consists of very
diverse elements. The bulk of the poem (6–37) is devoted
to the 'runes' and the precepts which Sigrdrífa gives to
Sigurðr. These (with the exception of str. 15, 16 and 17,
which contain lists and are in *fornyrðislag*) are in *lióðaháttr*
metre. The first section is partly in prose, partly in *fornyrðislag* and partly in *lióðaháttr* and relates the finding of
Sigrdrífa by Sigurðr. As in the *Hávamál* the nature of the
subject-matter would permit of numerous additions, and
scholars disagree as to which strophes are original and which
interpolations. Mogk[2] considers the *rúnar* strophes and the
precepts to be the kernel of the poem: Müllenhoff[3] the non-
didactic strophes 2, 3, 4, 5, 20, and 21; while F. Jónsson[4]
would exclude the *rúnar* strophes from the original poem but
include the precepts.

With regard to the date of the trilogy, all scholars
agree that the poems date from pre-Christian times—and
some would put *Reginsmál* and *Fáfnismál* very early. The
home of the poems seems most probably to have been
Norway.

---

[1] For a discussion of the relationship between the Edda version and the
Völsunga Saga, cp. F. Jónsson, I. pp. 280 ff.
[2] *Op. cit.* p. 632.
[3] *Deutsche Altertumskunde,* 1883, v. pp. 160 f.
[4] *Op. cit.* I. pp. 279 ff.

The poem *Grógaldr* is preserved only in paper MSS[1] dating from the latter half of the seventeenth century, and in most of these we find the title *Gróu galdr er hon gól syni sínum dauð*. The title *Svipdagsmál*, commonly applied to it and *Fjölsvinnsmál*, is not found in any MS conjointly, but was introduced by Bugge in his Excursus on the poems[2]. That the two poems originally belonged together was first conjectured by Grundtvig and Bugge from a comparison with Danish and Swedish ballad versions, preserved in MSS of those from the sixteenth and seventeenth centuries, in which the themes of *Grógaldr* and *Fjölsvinnsmál* are to be found combined to form one whole. These ballad versions however, although clearly treating the same theme, do not help to elucidate the obscurities of the *Grógaldr*. The spell-song which is the main feature of the *Grógaldr* is omitted in the ballad versions.

With regard to the date of the poem there is considerable difference of opinion. F. Jónsson and Mogk, quoting the reference to the dead Christian woman in str. 13, suggest the early eleventh or late tenth centuries. On the other hand Falk and Heusler[3] attribute it to the thirteenth century. Both the former scholars think that it originated in Norway; but Mogk regards its present form as Icelandic.

---

[1] I have not attempted to distinguish the readings of the various MSS. For information on this subject, see the editions of the Edda, especially Bugge, pp. xliv f., 338 ff., and Sijmons, xiii f., 196 ff.; Gering, pp. 193 ff.

[2] *Sæmundar-Edda*, pp. 352 ff.

[3] *Ark. f. nord. Filologi*, Vol. v (1893), p. 331; *Arch. f. d. Stud. d. neueren Sprachen*, Vol. 116, p. 266.

IV. THE GNOMIC MATERIAL OF THE EDDA

The bulk of the gnomic material of the Edda is to be found in the *Hávamál*, str. 1–95, 102 and 103, 111–137. Of the remainder a series of sixteen strophes is contained in the *Sigrdrífumál* and a series of six strophes in the *Reginsmál*. The last series has been included here with the rest of the gnomic material inasmuch as it embodies the advice given by Hnikarr (Óðinn) to Sigurðr, though this is based on magic rather than on common sense. Elsewhere however we find the two elements overlapping[1].

All these strophes are printed and translated below (pp. 44–99), while the rest of the gnomic material in the Trilogy and in the remaining Edda poems is introduced incidentally in this chapter. It is proposed now to make a brief examination of this material with a view to ascertaining the nature of the philosophy it expounds. In order the more easily to compare and contrast it, we may classify it under certain headings and arrange it in the following order:

I A. *Hávamál* 1–95, I B. *Hávamál* 111–137 (the *Loddfáfnismál*), II. *Sigrdrífumál*, III. *Reginsmál* (Hnikarr's advice), IV. The remaining gnomic material in the *Reginsmál* and the *Fáfnismál*, V. Gnomic material in the mythological poems, VI. Gnomic material in the heroic poems.

I A. The *Hávamál* 1–95 contains the longest series of precepts. Here the classification is based on the order in which the precepts are presented. Roughly speaking they may be grouped in the following way :

A. Maxims dealing with social intercourse between host and guest, host and stranger, guest and guest.

B. Precepts dealing with friendship and enmity.

C. Precepts and Maxims of a general character, especially such as relate to qualities which make for success in life.

---

[1] Cp. *Háv.* 137, with the rest of the *Loddfáfnismál*.

D. Reflections on the relationship between man and woman.

It will be seen that all four sections deal with man in his relationship to society. A, B and D however emphasise special aspects of this relationship, while C gives generally those qualities which a man should possess if he desires to have a good reputation among his fellows. A hard and fast line cannot always be drawn between these divisions.

Most of the gnomes which may be classed under A belong to str. 1–37, most of those under B to str. 41—52, most of those under C to str. 54–82, and most of those under D to str. 84–94. There is a certain amount of overlapping, and in some cases one may hesitate as to the class to which a gnome should be referred. But there can be no doubt that the general sequence is as indicated above. It will be convenient here to give a brief analysis of the gnomes contained in *Hávamál* str. 1–95.

A. *Social Intercourse.*

1. Maxims emphasising the value of caution, str. 1, 6, 7.

2. Maxims containing rules of etiquette, str. 2, 3, 4, 19[2,3,4], 33, 35, 36, 37 and 83[1].

3 a. Maxims enumerating desirable characteristics, str. 5, 8, 9, 10, 11[1,2], 63. (These advocate intelligence, independence and savoir faire in conversation.)

3 b. Maxims enumerating undesirable characteristics with their attendant penalties :
   (1) Drunkenness, 11[3,4], 12, 13, 14, 19[1].
   (2) Foolishness, 17, 24–27, 75[1,2].
   (3) Greediness, 20 and 21.
   (4) Scoffing, 22, 30, 31.
   (5) Chattering, 29, 65.
   (6) Quarrelling, 32.
   (7) Unpopularity, 62, 66, 67.

B. *Friendship and Enmity.*

Maxims giving the following advice :

1. Give gifts to friends, go and see them often, exchange ideas with them, str. 41, 42[1,2], 44.

2. Be cautious and crafty with those you distrust, $42^{3,4}$, $43^{3,4}$, 45, 46. Do not waste time visiting an untrustworthy friend, 34.

3. Strophes stating the need for and effects of friendship, str. 47, 49, 50, and 57.

4. Strophes stating the difference between true and false friendship, 51 and 52.

C. *General Precepts and Maxims.*

1. Maxims emphasising the value of moderation, 54, 55, 56, 64.

2. Precepts inculcating practical rules for everyday life, 58, 59, 60, 61 and $82^{1,2}$.

3. Health and reputation should be one's aim, $68^{3,4}$, 72, $76^{3,4}$, $77^{3,4}$.

4. The compensations of life, 69, 70, 71, 72.

5. The mutability of life and its inequalities, 53, $75^{3,4}$, $76^{1,2}$, $77^{1,2}$, 78.

6. Maxims showing the necessity for caution and suspicion, 38, 73, 74, 81, 85, 89.

7. Definitive or functional maxims, $82^{3,4}$.

D. *Man's relationship to Woman.*

1. Precepts advising distrust of woman, str. 84, 90.

2. Precepts giving advice on the wooing of woman, str. 92.

3. General statements—man is faithless to woman (str. 91), love is irresistible (str. 93 and 94).

For a strophe to strophe examination of the above material and an attempt to show that it contains a coherent and developed argument, the reader is referred to F. Jónsson, I. pp. 225 ff. In order however to achieve his aim he assigns certain definite strophes to a later date than the original poem[1]. As this involves many difficult, and probably insoluble, problems, it is perhaps wiser to content oneself with a general classification and the remark that this part of the

---

[1] Cp. p. 7 above.

Hávamál in its extant form gives a consistent policy of life. In the strophes following (96–110) we find two episodes which are apparently intended as practical illustrations of the tenets dealing with man's relationship to woman.

I B. If we now turn to the *Loddfáfnismál* (str. 111–137) we find that although there seem to be groups of two and three strophes dealing with similar subject-matter, there is here certainly no connected or developed argument. The strophes however, with the exception of six, are all linked, inasmuch as each is introduced with a conventional formula *Ráðomk þér, Loddfáfnir*[1]. If we use the same classification as before we see that these precepts may be grouped as follows:

A. *Social Intercourse.*

(*a*) Precepts advocating hospitality, str. 132–136.

(*b*) The following precepts :
Do not confide in a bad man, str. 117.
Do not exchange words with a fool, str. 122 and 123.
Do not bandy words with an inferior, str. 125.

B. *Friendship and Enmity.*

(i) Go and see good friends, give them gifts, confide in them, 119–121, 124.

(ii) Give no peace to your enemies, 127[5].

(iii) A statement that a confidant is a necessity, 121[6,7].

C. *General Precepts and Maxims.*

1. Precepts inculcating practical rules, 116, 126.
2. Precepts inculcating caution, 112, 131.
3. Precepts advising one not to rejoice in evil, 128.
4. Precepts advocating a policy of moderation, 131.

In addition we find two strophes based on a belief in magic, str. 129 and 137.

D. *Man's relationship to Woman* (precepts couched in the form of commands):

1. Distrust a woman who is skilled in magic, str. 113, 114.
2. Woo a worthy woman with flattery and gifts, str. 130.

---

[1] Cp. for similar formulae, *Sigrdr.* 22 ff.

3. Have nothing to do with the wife of another man, str. 115.

4. A statement that the tongue of an evil woman can bring about the death of a man, str. 118.

A comparison of these two sets of strophes (I A and I B) shows that they have certain precepts in common. Str. 130[1] has something in common with str. 92; str. 119[2] and 124 with str. 44, for in each we are told to confide in our friends and go to see them often; str. 121 with str. 47 and 50, for in each the statement is made that friendship is necessary to a human being.

In contradistinction to this, the *Loddfáfnismál* recognises both in its vocabulary and as the basis of at least three of its precepts the existence and power of magic—an element practically absent from the first series of strophes. We find for example such words as *fjölkunnigr, heilla*—and others like *eyrarún, gamanrún* and *líknargaldr* which originated in magic, even if in the *Loddfáfnismál* they are not used with all the force of their original meaning. In addition str. 113 and 129 are both based on the belief that men can be paralysed by the might of magic, while str. 137 appears to be an old magical receipt.

One further point may be noted in a contrast between the two series of strophes. In the first set, the adjectives good and evil (*góðr, illr*) are not applied to persons except ironically. We find good and evil friends mentioned, but apparently the adjectives describe the quality of the friendship and not the character of the person concerned. In the *Loddfáfnismál* on the other hand we have at least five references to good and bad men and women. The good are to be cultivated, the bad avoided[3]. Although the contrast should not be pressed too far—inasmuch as the exact force of such adjectives is difficult to determine—I would suggest that the emphasis in the first set of strophes is laid more clearly on the clever man as contrasted with the fool, whereas

---

[1] Cp. also *Háv.* 161.
[2] The wording of these strophes is also very similar.
[3] Cp. str. 117, 123, 130, 133.

in the *Loddfáfnismál* it would seem that moral worth was recognised as well as intellectual[1]. The general sentiments however of the two sets are very similar.

II. From the *Hávamál* we turn to the *Sigrdrífumál* which contains the greatest amount of gnomic material in the Trilogy. In str. 22 ff. Sigrdrífa, the valkyrie, gives Sigurðr wise counsel. All precepts, with the exception of five[2], are prefixed by the formula *Ðat ræð ek þér it fyrsta,...annat*, etc. There is however no developed or connected argument.

Do not contend with a fool (and the consequences), str. 24, 25.

Do not be involved in a drunken brawl, str. 29, 30.

Beware of evil from friends, str. 37[1,2].

Do not trust enemies, str. 35.

Be long-suffering with your relations, however provoking, str. 22.

Do not swear falsely, str. 23.

Be cautious and shun those who are treacherous, str. 32[1,2].

A prince should have his wits and weapons at hand, str. 36[3,4].

Pay due rites to the unburied dead, str. 33, 34.

Beware of the woman skilled in magic, str. 26, 27.

Be careful in your dealings with women, str. 28, 32[3,4].

It will be seen from this that the *Sigrdrífumál* has certain precepts in common with the *Hávamál*. Both poems advise one not to dispute with a fool (*Sigrdr.* 24, *Háv.* 122); to be on guard against enemies (*Sigrdr.* 35 f., and *Háv.* 89), against drink (*Sigrdr.* 29[4], *Háv.* 13[2]), and against women skilled in magic (*Sigrdr.* 26, 27 and 28, *Háv.* 113, 114).

In addition to such similarities it will also be observed that the general attitude towards life expressed in the poem is very similar to that expressed in the *Loddfáfnismál*, and it would seem as if many of the precepts uttered by the

---

[1] It must be noted however that str. 123 suggests that evil and stupidity are to be regarded as identical. F. Jónsson regards this strophe as an interpolation.

[2] Str. 25, 27, 30, 34 and 36 merely amplify the preceding strophe.

valkyrie are drawn from current philosophy[1]. There are however certain new elements which require explanation. For such precepts as those contained in str. 22, 23, 32[1,2], 35, and 37[1,2], F. Jónsson[2] would refer to the history of Sigurðr's life. But even if we accept this explanation[3] it could not account for such strophes as 33 and 34 which demand that due respect should be paid to an unburied body[4].

III. Before proceeding to a consideration of the incidental gnomic material of the *Reginsmál* and the *Fáfnismál*, the strophes embodying Hnikarr's advice to Sigurðr must be briefly commented upon. In reply to the latter's question— " What are the best omens amid the clash of arms, if one has to fight?"—Hnikarr enumerates six; four are based on superstition, one appears to be rational, while strophe 25[1,2] gives advice reminiscent of the *Hávamál* 61[1,2]. Two of these strophes are characterised by similar literary formulae to that found in the *Hávamál* 147 ff. Strophe 23 is unique in that it is in *fornyrðislag* and not in *lióðaháttr* metre.

IV. Apart from Hnikarr's advice there are only two strophes in the *Reginsmál* which contain gnomic material. Both occur in the story told by Reginn to Sigurðr. In str. 4 we are told of the penalty for perjury[5]; in str. 10 the dying Hreiðmarr ejaculates " *mart er, þat er þörf þear!* " which appears to mean " Necessity knows no law ! "

In the *Fáfnismál* all the gnomic precepts may be classed under one of three headings, those dealing with moderation, those with courage and those with fate. The first are contained in strophes 17 and 24[6] and echo the sentiment of *Hávamál* 64—that no man is the boldest when he mixes

---

[1] Str. 24, 26, 27, 28[4], 29[4], 30, 31, 32, 36[3,4].
[2] I. pp. 281 ff.
[3] Cp. however for str. 23 the *Völuspá* 39.
[4] Cp. the *Grágás*, II, LXI.
[5]   *ósaðra orða hverr er á annan lýgr,*
                   oflengi leiða limar.
   Cp. *Völuspá* 39 and *Norges Gamle Lǫv*, II. 426.
[6] *Fáfnismál* 17,

         Ægishjalmr   bergr einugi,
         hvar er skolo vreiðir vega;
      þá þat finnr   er með fleirom kǫmr,
         at engi er einna hvatastr.

with other bold men. Courage is advocated in strophes 30 and 31 as being of more value than any weapon[1]. The aphorisms dealing with fate are to be found in strophes 10 and 11. The latter, apparently a proverb from construction, may be translated "Every spot is perilous for a doomed man[2]"; the former, "Every man wishes to retain possession of his property until one fixed day, for when his time comes every man must go hence to hell[3]." Three other strophes require consideration, for they seem to contain proverbs. This is certainly the case in strophe 7 which is preceded by the phrase "they say" and apparently means "They say a prisoner always trembles[4]." The proverbs in the two[5] preceding strophes are obscure in meaning. All three occur in the conversation between Fáfnir and Sigurðr— which at this point becomes very much like a flyting. Each opponent in turn seems to cap his retort with a proverb and it will be noted that in each case the proverb occurs in the last line of the strophe. We may note here that this appears

Fáfnismál 24,
   Ðat er óvist at vita,   *þá er komom allir saman*
   sigtiva synir,
   hverr óblauðastr er alinn;
   margr er sd hvatr,   *er hjör ne rýðr*
   annars brjóstom í.

[1] *Fáfnismál* 30[1,2],
   Hugr er betri   *en sé hjörs megin,*
    hvar er reiðir skolo vega.
Fáfnismál 31,
   Hvötom er betra   *an sé óhvötom*
    í hildileik hafaz;
   glöðom er betra   *an sé glúpnanda*
    hvat sem at hendi kømr.

[2] *Allt er feigs forað.* An interesting modification of the same idea is to be found in the *Málsháttakvæði* 25—*sjaldan hittisk feigs vök frærin.*

[3] *Fáfnismál* 10,
   Fé ráða   *vill fyrða hverr*
   is til ins eina dags,
   þviat eino sinni   *skal alda hverr*
    fara til heljar heðan.

[4] *Æ kveða bandingja bifaz.*

[5] *Fáfnismál* 5. The MS reads *aburnno skjor a skeið.* For the various explanations and emendations cp. Edda, Hildebrand Gering, 1912, p. 303, and Detter and Heinzel, p. 410.

Fáfnismál 6,
   Fár er hvatr   *er hrørar tekr*
    ef í barnæsko er blauðr.
Cp. *Völsunga S.*: *fár er gamall harðr, ef hann er í bernsko blautr,* and *Hugsvinnsmál, þvi skal ungur venjast sem gamall skal fremja.*

to be a common use of proverbs—both in verse and prose. We may compare *Hárbarðsljóð* 22 and *Grettis S.* 21.

V. *Incidental gnomic material in the mythological poems.*

Scattered throughout the mythological poems of the Edda one finds an occasional strophe, half-strophe or line containing gnomic material. These are as follows:

Vafþrúðnismál 10: "A needy man who comes to a wealthy man should say what is needful or be silent. I think excessive talking will get sorry payment for him who comes on a visit to a cunning man[1]."

Lokasenna 47[3,4]: "For excessive drinking overpowers every man and makes him heedless of his chattering[2]."

Alvíssmál 3: "Let no man break his pledged word[3]."

Skírnismál 13[1,2]: "Other expedients are better than whining for him who is prepared for a journey."

In addition to the above there is an obscure proverb[4] in the *Hárbarðsljóð* 22, while *Lokasenna* 31 and *Skírnismál* 13[3,4] contain verbal reminiscences of the *Hávamál*. The obscure last line of the *Grógaldr* 4 also appears to be gnomic and is translated by F. Jónsson (*s.v.* skeika) as *Skuld går ifølge skæbnen* ("fate works according to destiny[5]").

VI. *Incidental gnomic material in the Heroic Poems of the Edda.*

1. *Brot* 11. "Vengeance shall be exacted for vindictive thoughts[6]." (Doubtful.)

---

[1] *Óauðugr maðr   er til auðugs kømr,*
    mæli þarft eða þegi;
    ofrmælgi mikil   hygg ek at illa geti,
    hveim er við kaldrifiaðan kømr.   *Vafþrúðnismál* 10.
[2] *þvíat ofdrykkja   veldr alda hveim,*
    er sína mælgi né manat.   *Lokasenna* 47[3,4].
[3] *bregði engi fösto heiti fira.*   *Alvíssmál* 3.
[4] *þat hefir eik   er af annarri skefr,*
    um sik er hverr í slíko.
The same proverb occurs in *Grettis Saga* XXI and in the *Málshátta kvæði* 26.
[5] *ok skeikar þá Skuld at sköpom.* Most editors however emend *skuld* to *skuldar.*
[6] *Heiptgjarns hugar   hefnt skal verða.*
    Brot af Sigurðarkviðo 11.

2. *Hamðismál* 8. "So ought every man to use a sorely wounding sword against the life of others that he does not harm himself[1]."

3. *Atlamál* 48. "No one can withstand fate[2]." (Cp. *Krakumál* 24.)

4. *Grípisspá* 53. "One cannot contend with fate[3]."

5. *Oddrúnargrátr* 34. "Every man lives according to his disposition[4]."

6. *Helreið Brynhildar* 14. "Far too long do both men and women strive to keep themselves alive in the face of overwhelming trouble[5]."

7. In the *Atlakviða* 19[6] and 31[7] we have two moral reflections on the part of the author of the poem—a type of reflection which does not occur elsewhere in the Edda; "Thus shall a brave man defend himself against his foes." "Thus shall a brave prince defend his gold against (other) men."

It will be seen that most of the gnomes contained in the last list belong to types which are of common occurrence in heroic poetry. We may compare the following passages from *Beowulf* (l. 455): "Fate will ever take the course it must"; (l. 1384 ff.) "For everyone it is nobler to avenge his friend than to indulge in excessive grief. Every one of us will have to face the end of human life"; (l. 1534 ff.) "Thus ought a man to act when he is minded to win lasting glory in battle"; (l. 2708 f.) "Such should a knightly follower be in the hour of need." Even the introductory formulae (e.g. *svá skal...*) are sometimes identical with those employed in the Anglo-Saxon poem.

The gnomes contained in the previous lists (I—V) are of a totally different character. Parallels may sometimes be found

---

[1] *Svá skyldi hverr öðrom   verja til aldrlaga*
sverði sárbeito   at sér né stríddit.   Ham. 8.
[2] *Sköpom viðr manngi.*   Atlamál 48.
[3] *Munat sköpom vinna.*   Gríp. 53.
[4] *Maðr hverr lifir at munom sínom.*   Odd. 32.
[5] *Muno við ofstríð   allz til lengi*
kono ok karlar   kvikvir forðaz (fœðaz).   Helreið 14.
[6] *Svá skal frœkn   fjándom verjaz....*   Atlak. 19.
[7]   *Svá skal gulli*
frœkn hringdrifi við fira halda.   ib. 31.

in the Anglo-Saxon gnomic verses contained in the Chronicle and the Exeter Book; but the tone of the Anglo-Saxon gnomes, in so far as they are not merely definitive, is as a rule either heroic or Christian. Better analogies may be found in the 'wisdom' literature of other nations, e.g. the Book of Proverbs, Hesiod's *Works and Days* and the Instructions of King Cormac MacAirt. But the Norse poems have a distinct individuality; the 'wisdom' which they contain is for the most part worldly wisdom of an exceptionally practical character. It is in the first part of the *Hávamál* that this is most conspicuous, and here, though proverbial wisdom of the more usual kind is by no means wanting, it is set off from time to time by touches of cynicism. In short the attitude of the poets is more sophisticated than is generally the case in this kind of literature.

What then are the cardinal virtues of the Eddic philosophy? They are caution and foresight, self-interest, moderation, independence, and savoir faire in conversation, while in the first ninety-five strophes of the *Hávamál* emphasis is laid on the importance of intelligence and common sense.

Of moral[1] sanctions such a philosophy is practically destitute. In the *Loddfáfnismál, Sigrdrífumál* and *Reginsmál* (Hnikarr's advice) the power of magic is recognised, but otherwise the penalties enumerated are merely the logical outcome of conduct. There is no mention of an obligation to civil law[2]; and the sanction of tradition and custom is barely recognised, for utility, not sentiment, is the test applied to action. The almost invariable test of conduct is public opinion and worldly success[3], though independence of judgment is most highly prized.

It may not be out of place here to ask how far the moral standards of this philosophy are exemplified by the actions of the men of the Viking Age. The Sagas of Icelanders (*Íslendinga sögur*) present us with a number of character

---

[1] Cp. however *Reginsmál* 4 and *Sigrdr.* 23.

[2] *Sigrdr.* 33 and 34 seem to be a relic of an old religious custom. The rites however are embodied in the *Grágás.*

[3] Cp. *Hávamál* 5, 8, 62, 66, 67, 76, 77, etc.

sketches of men of that period drawn in clear lines, and these portraits present a great variety of features. We find (especially in the early part of the period) men like Thórolfr of Mostr who are evidently sincerely religious, and on the other hand we hear from the beginning of those who "trusted in their own might and strength." Among the latter we may doubtless count the famous Egill Skallagrímsson whose character exhibits not a few of the traits commended in our poems, though perhaps a better illustration is afforded by the half-religious Víga-Glúmr. But the most striking illustration of this philosophy is probably to be found in the character of Snorri, the Priest, a great-grandson of Thórolfr of Mostr and one of the most influential men in Iceland at the beginning of the eleventh century.

The caution and foresight so necessary in the *Hávamál* for the would-be successful man characterise Snorri's actions from the first. Even as a lad of fifteen years he does not waste his money on fine clothes and smart horses[1], but saves it until an opportunity presents itself for him to claim his father's heritage from his uncle. The description of Snorri in cap. xv. of the *Eyrbyggja Saga* as master of the estate he had obtained by his astuteness is worth quoting: "In his daily life he was of an equable temperament and one could rarely ascertain whether he was pleased or not[2]. He was a wise man and far-sighted, but unforgiving and vindictive. The advice which he gave his friends was helpful: those who were not his friends could not repress a shudder at his plans[3]."

His independence of judgment and his worldly wisdom make his neighbours and his friends appeal to him constantly for advice, and although his conversations are not generally given verbatim it is clear throughout the sagas how frequently his advice was taken. It was Snorri who hatched the plot to save Styrr's daughter[4] and it was he who gave Guðrún

---

[1] *Eyrbyg. S.* xiii, and cp. *Háv.* 61.
[2] His reserve and control over his feelings is well shown in cap. xliv. When his kinsman Már was slain, Snorri's only comment was: "It is well to notice that it is not always best to be last."
[3] *Eyrbyg. S.* xv.   [4] Cp. *Eyrbyggja S.* xxviii.

shrewd counsel when she wished to avenge her husband Bolli's death[1].

His implacability to his foes is again and again illustrated, whether he uses physical force and slays his victim as in the case of Vigfúss who plotted against his life[2], or more frequently when he uses guile to rid himself of a troublesome person, as in the case of Björn[3], for he is no believer in physical force if it can be avoided.

The strength of Snorri's position partly lay in his unfailing realisation of exactly how far he could go. The moderation advocated in the *Hávamál* is part of his philosophy—but his motives for any such apparent virtue are never in doubt. If he makes a generous truce with his foes it is either because he sees their reinforcements approaching, or because for his own sake he does not wish the matter brought up at the *althingi*[4]. It was this same moderation which urged him to speak against the continued outlawry of Grettir[5], "who," he shrewdly remarked, "could do so much mischief that many would suffer for it."

Our prose authorities for this period are almost wholly of Icelandic origin, and consequently we have not the same detailed information for Norwegian society, but it cannot be doubted that this type of character existed in the motherland also—indeed there are hints of it even in the stories of some of the first settlers. These persons were largely drawn from the landowning class. In many cases they were the sons of *hersar*, and as such they had frequent opportunities of travel and even some acquaintance with court life. But the poetry itself cannot be described as of court origin, although it is for the most part put in the mouth of Óðinn, the god of royalty. This attribution however is probably to be connected with the fact that Óðinn constantly figures in the poems of persons—even in Iceland—who otherwise doubtless gave little heed to his worship.

---

[1] *Laxdœla S.* LIX.　　　　　　[2] *Eyrbyggja S.* XXVI.
[3] *Eyrbyggja S.* XLIII.　　　　[4] *Eyrbyggja S.* LVI.
[5] *Grettis Saga,* IV. LI.

V. THE MYTHICAL MATERIAL OF THE HÁVAMÁL

There are two sections of the *Hávamál* poem which deal with mythical subjects—one telling the story how Óðinn procured the mead, the other describing how he acquired the "runes." The former is preceded in the text by a story very similar to it in both style and subject-matter—the story of Óðinn's adventure with the daughter of Billingr[1]—and this in turn is preceded by a number of precepts on the relationship between men and women.

The story of Billingr's daughter (str. 96–102) is told vividly in a conversational style with humour and dramatic sense. The god is introduced lying hidden in the reeds, waiting to see the beautiful daughter of Billingr. In response to her suggestion he attempts to enter her house secretly, but finds the retinue of warriors awake in the hall and ready to give him a hostile reception. When he approaches a second time he finds the lady has played a trick on him by tying a dog to her bed-side. In str. 102 the moral of the story is drawn.

This adventure is followed by the mead myth[2] told in the same sprightly manner—perhaps to illustrate the precept (in str. 103) that a wise man ought to have an eloquent tongue, for it was only by this means that Óðinn achieved success in the halls of Suttungr. Only the outline of the story is given in the *Hávamál*; the details are filled in by Snorri in the *Bragarœður*—where the whole story of the mead-getting is told in response to the question of Ægir: "Whence did this art which you call 'poesy' derive its beginnings?" In the *Hávamál* we are told how Óðinn at the risk of his life, with the help of the auger Rati, pierced his way through the rocks till he came to the home of the giant Suttungr. The mead Óðrerir was in the keeping of Suttungr's daughter,

---

[1] Cp. *Saxo*, p. 363 ff.

[2] Grimm, *Deutsche Mythologie*, p. 873, has pointed out the similarity in the sequence of events between the 'Mead' myth and the 'Sampo' myth of the Kalewala. For the details of the myth, cp. Hastings, *Encyclopædia of Religion and Ethics*. *s.v.* 'Kalewala' 5.

Gunnlöð, to whom Óðinn made love and hence procured a drink. The concluding strophes of this section are devoted to Óðinn's self-congratulations on his achievement.

Apparent references to the same story are to be found in *Hávamál* 13 and 14, in which Óðinn mentions that he became drunk in the houses of Gunnlöð and Fjalarr. The latter name is not found in the *Hávamál* version of the story, but Snorri uses it in the *Bragarœður*[1].

It is in Snorri's version of the story that we find not only a description of the making of the precious mead but also details of Óðinn's escape from the halls of Suttungr. The former reads: "The gods had a dispute with a people called *Vanir* and arranged with them a peace meeting and made peace in this way: they each went to a vat and spat their spittle in it[2]. And at parting the gods took the peace token and would not let it perish, and created out of it a man. He was called Kvasir, and was so wise that no one could question him about things of which he did not know the answer; and he went up and down the earth to give instruction to men. And when he came, upon invitation, to certain dwarfs, Fjalarr and Galarr, they called him into secret conversation with them and slew him, letting his blood run into two vats and a kettle. The kettle is called Óðrerir but the vats Són and Boðn. They blended[3] honey with the blood and thus was made the mead, of the virtue of which he who drinks becomes a skald or a scholar."

With the latter part of this account one might perhaps compare the reference to Óðrerir in the *Hávamál* 140, and its effect on Óðinn, str. 141. In Snorri's version moreover we have the conclusion of the story given in detail. Snorri states that Óðinn assumed the guise of an eagle to make his escape

---

[1] *Skaldskaparmál* I.

[2] Cp. Grimm, *Deutsche Mythologie*, p. 902 transl. "atonements and treaties were often hallowed by mingling of bloods." Here the holy spittle is equivalent to blood.

[3] Frazer, *Golden Bough*, I. pp. 133 ff., gives cases of inspiration by the sucking of the fresh blood of a sacrificed victim; cp. Andrew Lang, *Myth, Ritual and Religion*, II. 173, "We are accustomed to hear in *Märchen* or peasant myths of Scotch, Russian, Zulu and other races, of drops of blood or spittle which possess human faculties and intelligence and which can reply for example to questions...."

from the halls of Suttungr. The latter started in pursuit, also in the shape of an eagle, and so hot was the chase that Óðinn was only just able to reach his goal and spit up the mead into the vats which the Æsir placed ready in their courts. Indeed so close was the pursuit that some of the mead did not reach the vats: " No heed however was paid to this, and any one who wished had it; we call that the poetasters' share."

It will be noticed that the *Hávamál* version of this story has many points in common with the story which precedes it—the episode of Billingr's daughter. Both stories too may be compared with Saxo's tale of Óðinn's wooing of Rinda, daughter of the king of the Ruthenians[1]. The following table summarizes what they have in common:

		Gunnlöð Story (Háv. 104 ff.)	*Billingr's daughter* *Story* (Háv. 96 ff.)	*Rinda Story* (Saxo)
1.	Hero	Óðinn	Óðinn	Óðinn
2.	Heroine	A reluctant lady	A reluctant lady	A reluctant lady
3.	Theme	Wooing	Wooing	Wooing
4.	Method	Crafty disguise	Stealth	Crafty disguise
5.	Object	To acquire the mead	No object mentioned	To enable Óðinn to avenge death of Balder
6.	Result	Success	A rebuff	Success.

Are these stories all versions of the mead myth—in two cases mutilated? A verse by Kormákr (quoted by Snorri in *Skaldsk.* II and LIV) possibly suggests that the Rinda story had to do with the mead. Moreover in a dirge by Ormr Steinðorsson occurs the kenning *Billings á burar full*, which Vigfusson and Powell interpret as a kenning for poetry, on the assumption apparently that the story of Billingr's daughter was a mead myth[2]. This however is but slight evidence, and may simply represent a misunderstanding of the story on the part of the skald.

Whatever the relationship between the two stories in the *Hávamál* (and the 'Rinda' story from Saxo), they are told with a humour and caustic wit which shows an absolute lack of reverence for the deity. They are only amusing anecdotes and represent an attitude to the gods similar to that which is frequently found in the Homeric poems[3].

---

[1] Cp. Saxo, pp. 94 ff. [2] *C.P.B.* II. p. 322.
[3] Cp. *Odyssey*, VIII. l. 265 ff.

But the belief underlying the story—that inspiration was originally due to the acquisition of a wonderful drink, the Óðrerir—finds an interesting parallel in the Soma cult of the Vedic mythology[1]. There we find constant mention of the Soma, a sacred plant, the juice[2] of which had certain miraculous properties. Not only was it used for medicinal purposes, but it was thought to have the power to confer immortality. Moreover it stimulated the voice and so became known as *vācas pati*—lord of speech or leader of speech. It was credited also with many other qualities, for we find the following epithets applied to it—lord of thought, leader and generator of hymns, leader of poets, a seer. Although the plant cult was the basis of the *Soma* conception, it must be mentioned that a deity was given the same name. A comparison of these characteristics with the features of the Óðrerir belief shows how much they have in common; the most striking similarity however is to be found in the myths telling of the acquisition of the drink. The bringing of the plant (the drink in Norse myth) from the mountains to the home of the gods is common to both mythologies. In both cases it is said to have been carried by an eagle and the fact that the god Indra is called an eagle on one occasion in connection with the *Soma* seems to indicate that here too we have the god in disguise as in the Scandinavian story[3]. The fact that a similar cult— that of the *Haoma*—is found in the Avesta suggests that the belief belonged to a time before the Indians and Iranians were divided.

For an interesting account of a similar modern belief the reader may be referred to Carl Lumholtz's *Unknown Mexico*[4], where there is a description of the plant called *hikuli*. It was much venerated by the Huichol Indians because it caused ecstasy when eaten. Other Mexican tribes ascribe to it the power of conferring health, long life and immunity from witchcraft.

---

[1] A. A. Macdonell, *Bühler's Grundriss*, p. 104, 'Vedic Mythology.'

[2] Not only the pure juice was used, but the juice sweetened with honey and mixed with milk and barley. In the Soma cult this was known as the *somyam madhu* ('soma mead').

[3] Cp. Macdonell, *Bühler's Grundriss*, p. 111. He also gives a comparison between the *Haoma* of the Avesta and the *Soma*.

[4] Carl Lumholtz, *Unknown Mexico*, i. p. 357.

The myth describing Óðinn's acquisition of the runes is embodied in str. 138 ff., and owing to its obscurity many diverse attempts have been made to explain it. The first problem is the difficulty presented by the sequence of the strophes. Is one considering logically connected strophes or disconnected fragments? Str. 138 gives a picture of Óðinn hanging for nine nights and stabbed with a spear, an offering to himself. Parallels in northern literature to the ritualistic and mythical details of this strophe have been given in the notes: for a strikingly similar sacrifice by hanging and stabbing combined we have the story of King Vikarr in *Gautreks Saga* VII: "Then he said to the king: 'Here is a gallows ready for you, O king, and I do not think it looks very dangerous.' The king climbed on to the stump, and Starkaðr laid the noose round his neck and leaped down. Then he thrust against the king with his cane, saying, 'Now I give thee to Óðinn,' and released the branch. The cane turned into a javelin and transfixed the king, the stump fell from beneath his feet and the strings turned into strong withies: the branch flew back and swept the king into the tree-top, and there he died[1]."

If str. 139 is to be connected with str. 138, are we to infer that the victim was starved in addition to the hanging and stabbing? Did this starvation take place before the hanging? If so, *sældo* would have to be taken as pluperfect tense, and similar difficulty would arise over the tense of *nýsta, nam ek, fell ek.* Moreover with what does *œpandi* agree, with *ek* or with *rúnar*? Finally, is the acquisition of the runes connected with the sacrifice mentioned in the preceding strophe and, if so, why should runes be found beneath a gallows?

If however str. 139 stands by itself, then the first line might perhaps be compared with the first line in *Grímnismál*, str. 2—

svá at mér manngi   mat né bauð,

but it is not easy to see how this passage bears on the rest of str. 139.

---

[1] Transl. Chadwick, *Cult of Othin*, p. 4.

If str. 140 is a true continuation of str. 139, are the *nío fimbulljóþ* which Óðinn obtains, together with a drink of Óðrerir, to be connected with the acquisition of the runes in str. 139?

Similarly, does str. 141 continue 140 with *þá* as the connecting word, and if so is the vocabulary of str. 141 to be compared with that of *Rígsþula* 22, which refers to physical growth? Can str. 141 mean mental rather than physical power—which is begotten and increased by the drink Óðrerir?

If str. 142 belongs to str. 141, can it be that the benefits acquired by the god are now to be bestowed on men—on the man who pays attention: *Heilir þeirs hlýddo!* Or are the strophes quite unconnected?

The same double possibility confronts one with str. 144. Is the ritual suggested in str. 144 connected with the runes of the preceding strophes? Its vocabulary would seem to link it with the obscure str. 145—the last line of which is also reminiscent of str. 139.

Finally, it is not only the details and sequence of these strophes which offer difficulties, but the significance of the whole passage is far from clear. If the strophes referred to form a connected whole, what are the elements which have gone to make up so obscure and complex a conception?

Why was Óðinn, a god, sacrificed to Óðinn? This question I do not think we are yet in a position to answer. To a certain extent parallels are to be found among the ancient Mexicans[1]. In all these cases however the victim is a human being, although he is identified with the god to whom he is offered. Can the idea of replenishing the life of the deity, which apparently underlies the Mexican ritual, be the root idea here? If we are to assume that the explanation lies along these lines, then it would seem as if the rite had fallen into abeyance and that only reminiscences of it remained when the poem was composed; otherwise it is difficult to account for the absence of any reference to a human person. The fact that the tree on which he is hanged is the world tree would seem to point in this direction.

---

[1] Frazer, *Golden Bough*, 'The Scapegoat,' cap. VII and elsewhere.

The word *rún* is used in Norse, as in Anglo-Saxon[1], in two different senses: (1) a letter of the native alphabet which was in use before the introduction of the Roman alphabet, and (2) a secret or mystery. The latter is no doubt the original meaning of the word since we find it in this sense not only in Gothic but also in Celtic languages, e.g. Gael. *rún*, 'secret'; Welsh *rhin*, 'secret,' 'charm' (cp. Greek ἐρευνάω, 'to search,' 'seek for'). The application of the word to writing is no doubt a survival of the time when the art of writing was new or only known to a few[2]. The use of the word *ráða* ('read,' lit. 'interpret') in relationship to writing likewise no doubt comes down from the same period.

In Norse literature the two meanings of the word *rún* are not always clearly distinguished—partly owing to the fact that runic letters were often used with a magical significance. This is one of the passages where the use of the word is far from clear[3].

What are these runes which Óðinn obtained by suffering? Is there any significance in their being found beneath the gallows? A belief that not only the dead body on the gallows but its droppings had special virtues[4] is common in folk-lore. Sir W. Ridgeway mentions[5] a custom of an Australian tribe based on a similar belief. Elsewhere[6] this belief seems to be closely connected with the herb mandrake. Can any light be thrown on the *Hávamál* passage by comparing it with the ritual connected with the pulling of herbs[7]?

---

[1] Bosworth and Toller, *Anglo-Saxon Dictionary*, *s.v.*

[2] We may compare *Iliad* vi. ll. 168 f., "and gave him tokens of woe, graving in a folded tablet many deadly things...." It is clear that the poet does not understand these tokens.

[3] A not inconsiderable number of runic inscriptions are still undeciphered and it is likely enough that these were intended to be used for magical purposes.

[4] Cp. Adam of Bremen, iv. 27 : *Is enim lucus* (at Upsala) *tam sacer est gentilibus ut singulae arbores ejus ex morte vel tabo immolatorem divinae credantur.*

[5] *Early Age of Greece*, p. 488.

[6] Frazer, *Folklore in the Old Testament*, ii. p. 381; Grimm, *Deutsche Mythologie*, p. 1202; Dasent, *Popular Tales from the North*, No. 1. For a story based on a similar superstition in modern times cp. Thomas Hardy, *Wessex Tales*, pp. 90 ff.

[7] Cp. O.H.G. *alruna*, i.e. mandrake; A.S. *dolh-rune*, i.e. pellitory.

VI. SPELL SONGS IN THE EDDA

In the three poems *Hávamál, Sigrdrífumál* and *Gró-galdr* we find spell songs, all of which are characterised by the repetition in each strophe of formulae. The spell songs in the *Hávamál*, generally known now as the *Lióðatal*[1], enumerate in eighteen strophes the situations over which Óðinn claims power by means of spells (*lióð*). In the *Ynglinga Saga* VI and VII Snorri gives what appears to be a paraphrase of this section of the *Hávamál* and ascribes to Óðinn the introduction of the black art into the north. "The reason for his (Óðinn's) renown was that he possessed the faculty of changing his countenance and figure in any way he wished.... In battle Óðinn had the power of making his foes blind or deaf or panic-stricken, while their weapons had no more effect than wands. And his men fought without coats of mail and were mad as dogs or wolves. They bit into their shields and were strong as bears or bulls. They slaughtered other people but no fire or steel had any effect on them....Óðinn was in the habit of changing his shape. His body would then lie as if asleep or dead, but he in reality had become a bird or beast, fish or snake, and had gone in a moment to a far off land on his own errands or those of other men. He alone knew how by certain words to cause a fire to be quenched, the sea to be calmed and the wind to change....At times he raised up dead men from the earth or sat under those who had been hanged."

In the *Sigrdrífumál* we find a valkyrie offering the young hero Sigurðr similar charms—called *rúnar*—which will give him power over certain difficulties. In the poem as we have it these are preceded by the offer of a magic drink. "I will bring to you, hero of the battle-field, beer mixed with might and powerful glory. It is full of spells and healing tokens, of beneficent charms and love runes[2]."

---

[1] Müllenhoff was the first to give the name.
[2] Str. 5   *Bjór fœri ek þér,   bryn þings apaldr!*
               magni blandinn   ok megintíri;
               fullr er hann ljóða   ok líknstafa,
               góðra galdra   ok gamanrúna.

These charms are repeated with slight alterations in the *Völsunga Saga* XX, and both in poem and saga not only is their virtue explained, as in the *Hávamál*, but the means needed to make them effective are described. In the *Rígs-ðula* 43 we are told that Konr had knowledge of *æfinrúnar* ('everlasting runes') and *aldrrúnar* ('life runes'), and in *Helgakviða Hundingsbana* II. 12 and 34 *valrúnar* ('runes of slaughter')[1] and *sakrúnar* ('runes of strife') are mentioned. The last are attributed to Óðinn.

A third series of spell songs (*galdrar*) are given in the *Grógaldr* str. 6–14 by Gróa to her son Svipdagr. Gróa is represented as chanting the spells within the portals of her cairn while standing "on a stone fixed in the ground[2]," in response to her son's request for help on a perilous journey. She concludes with the admonition—"Carry away with you, O son, the words of your mother and let them occupy your thoughts. Abundant good fortune will you always have so long as you remember my words." There are later versions of this story in Danish and Swedish ballads preserved in sixteenth and seventeenth century MSS[3], but they throw no light on the obscure passages of the poem. In them the hero's mother does not offer him charms but such things as a magic sword and a wonderful horse to help him on his way.

A comparison of the subject-matter of these three sets of spell songs shows that they have certain spells in common. Both Óðinn and Sigrdrífa claim to be able to heal the sick and to blunt an enemy's weapons. Óðinn and Gróa can loosen a prisoner's fetters, while all three have control over the weather. Finally both Sigrdrífa and Gróa understand and can bestow the runes of speech (*Sigrdr.* 12; *Gróg.* 14), a power attributed to Óðinn in the *Hyndluljóð* 3. From

---

[1] Cp. however Vigfusson, *s.v.*

[2] *á jarðföstom steini*, cp. Saxo, p. 16: "The ancients, when they were to choose a king, were wont to stand on stones planted in the ground, and to proclaim their votes, in order to foreshadow from the steadfastness of the stones that the deed would be lasting." For modern parallels, cp. Frazer, *Magic Art*, I. p. 160. Compare also the *Iliad*, XVIII. l. 504.

[3] Cp. Bugge, *Sæmundar-Edda*, pp. 352 ff.

incidents in the sagas it would seem that such were the claims commonly made by persons skilled in magic[1].

The three groups of spells described and compared above are all beneficent, i.e. beneficial to the person addressed. In the Edda however we also find maleficent spells—such as those uttered by Skírnir against Gerðr (*Skírnismál* 26 ff.). But these curses are of a special character determined by the occasion and do not contain what may perhaps be called the conventional and general subject-matter found in a varying degree in all the other three. They resemble rather Egill's curse against the *land-vættir*[2]. "He (i.e. Egill) took in his hand a hazel-pole and went on to a certain cliff....Then he took a horse's head and stuck it on the pole. After that he uttered an imprecation, speaking as follows: 'I set up here a *niðstöng* (a pole causing insult) and I turn this insult against King Eric and his queen Gunnhildr.' (He turned the horse's head towards the land.) 'I turn this insult against the *land-vættir* ('guardian spirits of the land') who dwell in this land, so that they may all wander astray and neither discover nor find their abode until they drive King Eric and Gunnhildr forth out of the land.'"

In the heroic poems of the Edda we find three sets of spell curses, the first uttered by Guðrún against Atli (*Atlakviða* 30), the second by Sigrún against Dagr (*Helgakviða Hundingsbana* II, 32), and the third by Vingi against himself—in case his oath prove false (*Atlamál* 33).

In all these spells, both beneficent and maleficent, the magic jargon, the allusions to obscure ritual and lost myth, the unfamiliarity of the superstitions, combined with the terse method of expression, make the strophes difficult to understand. In the notes I have tried to throw light on the obscure

---

[1] In early ecclesiastical literature both in England and elsewhere we find similar powers attributed to Christian saints. Cf. Bede, *H.E.* IV. cap. 22, and *pass.*

[2] *Hann tók í hönd sér heslistöng ok gekk á bergsnös nökkura...þá tók hann hrosshöfuð ok setti upp á stöngina. Síðan veitti hann formála ok mælti svá: 'Hér set ek upp niðstöng ok sný ek þessu niði á hönd Eiríki konungi ok Gunnhildi drotningu'—hann sneri hrosshöfuðinu inn á land—'Sný ek þessu niði á land-vættir þær er land þetta byggja svá at allar fari þær villar vegar, engi hendi né hitti sitt inni fyrr enn þær reka Eirík konung ok Gunnhildi ór landi.'* Egils S. LVII.

myth and ritual by illustrating wherever possible from other passages in Northern literature. The unfamiliarity of the superstition is often a serious difficulty, but a certain amount of assistance can be obtained from stories in which we find similar spells in actual use. A few words however must be said here on the magic jargon and in particular on the three most commonly used terms—*ljóð*, *rún* and *galdr*.

The word *ljóð* is used both in verse and prose to mean either a strophe from a song or poem, or the song or poem itself. In the *Hávamál* and the *Sigrdrífumál* however it certainly has a more technical meaning[1] and stands for a spell song or a charm which was to be chanted. In *Ynglinga S.* VII Snorri defines such *ljóð* as "those which are called *galdrar.*" The word *galdr* is identical with the A.-Sax. *galdor* and derived from *gala*, 'to sing,' but both in Anglo-Saxon and Norse it is generally used with the meaning 'incantation,' and we also find it employed in the sense of witchcraft. With this sense it is very frequently found in compounds. Adam of Bremen[2] may have been referring to incantations of the kind mentioned above when he says (speaking of the ritual celebrations at the temple of Upsala) "there are many kinds of these *neniae*, but they are unseemly and it is better therefore not to mention them."

With regard to *rún*, we have seen above (p. 37) that the word is used with two different meanings: (1) a letter of the alphabet, (2) a mystery, and that the two meanings are not clearly distinguished in the *Sigrdrífumál*. It is evident in some cases at least that letters are meant but that they are used with a magical rather than with a phonetic value. Examples of the use of such magical letters are given in the *Hávamál*, str. 80, 111, 137, 139, 142, 143, and in str. 144 we seem to have the ritual necessary for making them effective. The very close connection which was believed to exist between *rúnar* and *galdrar* is shown by a passage in a tract—*De Inventione Linguarum*—by Hrabanus Maurus, who was Abbot of Fulda and Archbishop of Mayence in the ninth century.

---

[1] Phillpotts, *Elder Edda*, pp. 55, 58, 81.
[2] Adam of Bremen, IV. 27, *neniae...multiplices et inhonestae ideoque melius reticendae.*

After giving an account of various kinds of writing he proceeds—" The letters also used by the Marcomanni (whom we call Northmen) we have written below. From these Northmen those who speak the German language are descended, and those who still follow heathen practices use these letters for the interpretation of their spell songs, incantations and divinations[1]."

An interesting comment on such runes is to be found in *Egils S.* LXXII, where Egill says: " No man ought to cut runes unless he knows quite clearly how to interpret them. It often happens to a man that he is bewildered by mysterious letters. I saw ten hidden runes on a bit of whale-bone which brought long enduring misery to a maiden." In *Skírnismál* 29 and 36 some of the names of these mysterious letters are given : *ergi, æði, óðoli, tópi, ópi, tjösull*[2]. Runic letters with phonetic value are also mentioned in the same connection—*Þurs*[3] in *Skírnismál* 36 and *Nauð* and *Týr* in the *Sigrdrífumál* 6 and 7.

In the *Sigrdrífumál* 15, 16 and 17 a list of objects is given on which runes may be inscribed, and it seems possible that such strophes may explain certain grave finds dating from as early as the Bronze Age. In the Magle-høi find the following things were found[4]—a horse's teeth, a weasel's bones, claws of a lynx, vertebræ of a snake, a bit of a bird's wind-pipe and pieces of sulphur, coal and bronze. It is difficult certainly to account for such a collection in any other way.

Moreover, the frequent mention in the Norwegian and Icelandic Laws of penalties imposed on those who make use of runes and spell songs shows that together with herbs and amulets these were the media by which magicians and witches worked their will on people. In Anglo-Saxon all three words are also preserved and the same close relationship between

---

[1] *Litteras quippe quas utuntur Marcomanni quos nos Nordmannos vocamus infra scriptas habemus: a quibus originem qui theodiscam loquuntur linguam trahunt: cum quibus* (i.e. *litteris*) *carmina sua incantationesque ac divinationes significare procurant qui adhuc paganis ritibus involvuntur.* Goldast, *Script. Rer. Alem.* II. Pt. i, p. 69.

[2] For conjectured meanings, cp. Egilsson, *s.v.* and Vigfusson, *s.v.*

[3] *Þurs, Nauð*(r), and *Týr* are the names of three letters in the Norse Runic alphabet.

[4] Described by V. Boye in *Aarbøger for nordisk Oldkyndighed og Historie,* Copenhagen, 1889, p. 317.

them is indicated by such a phrase as *rune writan, leoþ gesingan* in the Exeter Gnomic Verses ll. 139 f.

The story of the way in which the death of Grettir was encompassed is one of the most striking descriptions in the sagas of the use of both runes and spell songs. A certain old woman called Þuríðr, who was skilled in witchcraft, determined to bring misfortune on Grettir because he had hurled a stone at her and broken her thigh bone. The saga describes in detail her method of procedure: "She limped forth along by the sea, even as she had been directed, to where there lay before her the roots of a tree as big as one could lift on to one's shoulder. She examined the tree and bade them (i.e. the people with her) turn it over in her presence. It was as if it had been burnt and scraped on the other side. She had a little flat space cut where it had been scraped. Afterwards she took her knife and carved runes on the root and reddened them with her blood and said spells over them. She went widdershins round the tree and said over it mighty words. After that she had the tree shoved into the sea and said as above that that would be washed out to Drangey and bring disaster to Grettir[1]."

[1] *Grettis S.* LXXXI.

THE HÁVAMÁL

1 Gáttir allar,   áðr gangi fram,
  um skoðaz skyli,
  um skygnaz skyli;
  þvíat óvíst er at vita   hvar óvinir
  sitja á fleti fyrir.

2 Gefendr heilir!   Gestr er inn kominn:
  hvar skal sitja sjá?
  mjök er bráðr   sá er á bröndom[1] skal
  síns um freista frama.

3 Elz er þörf   þeims inn er kominn
  ok á kné kalinn;
  matar ok váða   er manni þörf
  þeim er hefir um fjall farit.

4 Vats er þörf   þeim er til verðar kømr,
  þerro ok þjóðlaðar,
  góðs um œðis,   ef sér geta mætti,
  orz ok endrþögo.

5 Vits er þörf   þeim er víða ratar;
  dælt er heima hvat;
  at augabragði verðr   sá er ekki kann
  ok með snotrom sitr.

6 At hyggjandi sinni   skylit maðr hrœsinn vera,
  heldr gætinn at geði:
  þá er horskr ok þögull   kømr heimisgarða til,
  sjaldan verðr víti vörom;
  þvíat óbrigðra vin   fær maðr aldregi
  en manvit mikit.

7 Inn vari gestr   er til verðar kømr,
  þunno hljóði þegir,
  eyrom hlýðir,   en augom skoðar;
  svá nýsiz fróðra hverr fyrir.

[1] **R**; á brautom pap. MSS.

THE HÁVAMÁL

1 Before making your way up the hall you should observe and note all the doorways, for you can never be certain when you will find enemies present.

2 Hail to the bountiful! A stranger has entered! Where is he to sit? He who has to prove his mettle at the hearth is in a great hurry.

3 A man who enters chilled to the very knees needs a fire. Food and clothing are needed by him who has been traversing the mountains.

4 He who comes for a meal requires water, a towel and a hearty welcome—a word of good cheer if he can get it, and polite attention.

5 A man who takes long journeys needs his wits about him: anything will pass at home. An ignorant man becomes an object of ridicule when he sits among the wise.

6 No man should be boastful about his intelligence but rather alert in his wits. When a man who is clever but reticent comes to a house his prudence often shields him from misfortune, for never will a man get a more trustworthy friend than a good store of common sense.

7 A cautious stranger who comes for a meal keeps silent with sharpened hearing—hearkens with his ears and watches with his eyes: so every wise man takes note of what is going on round him.

8 Hinn er sæll   er sér um getr
    lof ok líknstafi ;
    ódæla er við þat   er maðr eiga skal
    annars brjóstom í.

9 Sá er sæll   er sjálfr um á
    lof ok vit meðan lifir ;
    þvíat ill ráð   hefir maðr opt þegit
    annars brjóstom ór.

10 Byrði betri   berrat maðr brauto at
    en sé manvit mikit ;
    auði betra   þikkir þat í ókunnom stað,
    slíkt er válaðs vera.

11 Byrði betri   berrat maðr brauto at
    en sé manvit mikit ;
    vegnest verra[1]   vegra hann velli at
    en sé ofdrykkja öls.

12 Era svá gott,   sem gott kveða,
    öl alda sona ;
    þvíat færa veit,   er fleira drekkr,
    síns til geðs gumi.

13 Óminnis hegri heitir   sá er yfir ölðrom þrumir :
    hann stelr geði guma ;
    þess fugls fjöðrom   ek fjötraðr vark
    í garði Gunnlaðar.

14 Ölr ek varð,   varð ofröevi
    at ins fróða Fjalars ;
    því er ölðr batst[2]   at aptr of heimtir
    hverr sitt geð gumi.

15 Ðagalt ok hugalt   skyli þjóðans barn
    ok vígdjarft vera ;
    glaðr ok reifr   skyli gumna hverr,
    unz sinn bíðr bana.

---

[1] emend. Bugge; *vera*, **R.**
[2] emend. Bugge; *batstr*, **R.**

8 Happy is the man who wins for himself a reputation and popularity. It is an uncomfortable position for a man when he has to depend on the mind of another.

9 Happy is the man who by independent effort preserves his reputation and depends on his mother wit as long as he lives. For often has a man received evil counsel from the mind of another.

10 There is no better load that a man can carry along with him than a good store of common sense. In a strange place it will prove better than riches, and it is a means of existence to him who is destitute.

11 There is no better load that a man can carry along with him than a good store of common sense. No worse provision will he carry on his way than too deep a draught of beer.

12 The ale of the sons of men is not so good as they say: for the more a man drinks the less control he has of his wits.

13 There is a bird called the heron of forgetfulness which hovers over the ale-drinking; it robs a man of his wits. With the feathers of that bird was I fettered in the abode of Gunnlöð.

14 I became drunk, exceedingly drunk, at the house of wise Fjalarr. Ale-drinking is not good for any man unless he recovers his wits.

15 A man of princely birth should be reticent and thoughtful and bold in fighting. Every man should be glad and cheerful until he meets his death.

16 Ósnjallr maðr hyggz muno ey lifa,
    ef hann við víg varaz ;
    en elli gefr hánom engi frið,
    þótt hánom geirar gefi.

17 Kópir afglapi er til kynnis kømr,
    þylsk hann um eða þrumir ;
    allt er senn, ef hann sylg um getr ;
    uppi er þá geð guma.

18 Sá einn veit er víða ratar
    ok hefir fjölð um farit
    hverjo geði stýrir gumna hverr
    sá er vitandi er vits.

19 Haldit maðr á keri, drekki þó at hófi mjöð ;
    mæli þarft eða þegi.
    Ókynnis þess vár þik engi maðr,
    at þu gangir snemma at sofa.

20 Gráðugr halr, nema geðs viti,
    etr sér aldrtrega ;
    opt fær hlœgis, er með horskom kømr,
    manni heimskom magi.

21 Hjarðir þat vito nær þær heim skolo,
    ok ganga þá af grasi :
    en ósviðr maðr kann ævagi
    síns um mál¹ maga.

22 Vesall maðr ok illa skapi
    hlær at hvívetna :
    hitki hann veit er hann vita þyrpti,
    at hann era² vamma vanr.

23 Ósviðr maðr vakir um allar nætr
    ok hyggr at hvívetna :
    þá er móðr er at morni kømr :
    allt er víl sem var.

¹ emend. Rask ; máls, **R.**
² emend. Rask ; er, **R.**

16 A cowardly man thinks he will live for ever if he takes care to avoid fighting, but old age will give him no quarter though he be spared by spears.

17 When a noodle comes on a friendly visit he gapes and chatters or sits dumb. If he gets a drink, then very speedily the character of the man's mind is fully exposed.

18 It is only he who makes far journeys and has travelled extensively who knows what kind of mind any man possesses who has control of his wits.

19 No man should be the slave of the drinking cup, though he may drink mead in moderation. He should say what is wanted or hold his tongue. No man will accuse you of ill manners for going to bed early.

20 A greedy man will lay up for himself life-long trouble unless he has his wits about him. When a fool mixes with intelligent people, his gluttony always makes him an object of derision.

21 Cattle know when it is time to go home and then they leave their pasture, but a foolish man never knows the measure of his own appetite.

22 He is a wretched man and evil of disposition who scoffs at everything. He does not know what he ought to know—that he himself is not irreproachable.

23 He is a foolish man who lies awake all night and broods over everything. When morning breaks he is weary and all his trouble is the same as it was.

24 Ósnotr maðr   hyggr sér alla vera
   viðhlæjendr vini;
   hitki hann fiðr,   þótt þeir um hann fár lesi,
   ef hann með snotrom sitr.

25 Ósnotr maðr   hyggr sér alla vera
   viðhlæjendr vini;
   þá þat finnr,   er at þingi kømr,
   at hann á formælendr fá.

26 Ósnotr maðr   þikkiz allt vita,
   ef hann á sér í vá vero;
   hitki hann veit   hvat hann skal við kveða,
   ef hans freista firar.

27 Ósnotr maðr[1],   er með aldir kømr,
   þat er batst at hann þegi;
   engi þat veit   at hann ekki kann,
   nema hann mæli til mart.
   veita maðr   hinn er vetki veit,
   þótt hann mæli til mart.

28 Fróðr sá þykkiz   er fregna kann
   ok segja it sama;
   eyvito leyna   mego ýta sønir,
   því er gengr um guma.

29 Œrna mælir   sá er æva þegir
   staðlauso stafi;
   hraðmælt tunga,   nema haldendr eigi,
   opt sér ógott um gelr.

30 At augabragði   skala maðr annan hafa,
   þótt til kynnis komi;
   margr þá fróðr þikkiz,   ef hann freginn erat,
   ok nái hann þurrfjallr þruma.

31 Fróðr þikkiz   sá er flótta tekr,
   gestr at gest hæðinn;
   veita görla   sá er um verði glissir,
   þótt hann með grömum glami.

---

[1] add. Rask; om. R.

24 He is a foolish man who thinks all who smile at him are his friends. If sensible people show their dislike for him when he is in their company, he will not realise it.

25 He is a foolish man who thinks all who smile at him are his friends. He will discover when he comes into court that he has but few supporters.

26 He is a foolish man who thinks he knows everything if he secures safety in danger. He will not know what to answer if men test him with questions.

27 When a senseless man mixes with other people he had better keep silent. No one will know how ignorant he is unless he talks too much. An ignorant man will never know that he is talking too much.

28 He is considered well-informed who can both ask and answer questions. The sons of men can never be silent about the frailty of their fellows.

29 He who is never silent will make many aimless remarks. A glib tongue, unless checked by its owner, will often make music to his sorrow.

30 A man ought not to hold another up to ridicule when he is paying a friendly visit. Many a man will be considered wise if he is not asked any questions and will manage to rest undisturbed with a dry skin.

31 A stranger inclined to mock at other strangers will be considered wise if he beat a retreat. He who pokes fun at table never knows for certain that he is not making enemies by his jesting.

32 Gumnar margir   erosk gagnhollir,
   en at virði rekaz;
   aldar róg   þat mun æ vera:
   órir gestr við gest.

33 Árliga verðar   skyli maðr opt fáa,
   nema til kynnis komi:
   sitr ok snópir,   lætr sem sólginn sé,
   ok kann fregna at fá.

34 Afhvarf mikit   er til illz vinar,
   þótt á brauto búi;
   en til góðs vinar   liggja gagnvegir,
   þótt hann sé firr farinn.

35 Ganga skal¹,   skala gestr vera
   ey í einom stað;
   ljúfr verðr leiðr   ef lengi sitr
   annars fletjom á.

36 Bú er betra   þótt lítit sé:
   halr er heima hverr;
   þótt tvær geitr eigi   ok taugreptan sal,
   þat er þó betra en bœn.

37 Bú er betra   þótt lítit sé:
   halr er heima hverr;
   blóðugt er hjarta   þeim er biðja skal
   sér í mál hvert matar.

38 Vápnom sínom   skala maðr velli á
   feti ganga framarr;
   þvíat óvíst er at vita   nær verðr á vegom úti
   geirs um þörf guma.

39 Fannka ek mildan mann,   eða svá matar góðan,
   at ei væri þiggja þegit,
   eða síns féar   svá gjöflan²
   at leið sé laun, ef þegi.

¹ add. Copenhagen ed.; om. **R**.
² emend. Munch; strophe is defective in **R**; *svági örvan*, pap. **MS**.

32 Many men who are kindly disposed to one another will become abusive at table. Quarrels among strangers will ever be a source of strife to mankind.

33 A man should always get a meal early in the day unless he is going to visit a friend. He will sit and gobble and look as if he were famished and be unable to enter into conversation.

34 On getting to a bad friend's house, though he lives on your route, you will have gone far out of your way; but the roads that lead to a good friend's house—however far he may have gone—do not deviate from the direct route.

35 A visitor should depart and not always be in one place. A friend becomes a nuisance if he stays too long in the house of another.

36 A house of your own is better, though it is only a little one. Every man is a person of consequence at home. Even if you only have two goats and a cottage thatched with fibre it is better than begging.

37 A house of your own is better, though it is only a little one. Every man is a somebody at home. It is heartbreaking to have to beg food for yourself for every meal.

38 A man ought not to move an inch from his weapons when away from home, for it can never be known with certainty when he will need the use of his spear as he goes forth on his travels.

39 I have never found a man so generous and hospitable that he would not receive a present, nor one so liberal with his money that he would dislike a reward if he could get one.

40 Fjár síns,   er fengit hefr,
    skylit maðr þörf þola:
opt sparir leiðom   þats hefir ljúfom hugat;
    mart gengr verr, en varir.

41 Vápnom ok váðom   skolo vinir gleðjaz—
    þat er á sjálfom sýnst;
viðrgefendr ok endrgefendr erosk[1] lengst vinir,
    ef þat bíðr at verða vel.

42 Vin sínom   skal maðr vinr vera
    ok gjalda gjöf við gjöf;
hlátr við hlátri   skyli hölðar taka,
    en lausung við lygi.

43 Vin sínom   skal maðr vinr vera,
    þeim ok þess vin;
en óvinar síns   skyli engi maðr
    vinar vinr vera.

44 Veitstu, ef þú vin átt   þann er þú vel trúir,
    ok vill þú af hánom gott geta:
geði skaltu við þann blanda   ok gjöfom skipta,
    fara at finna opt.

45 Ef þú átt annan   þannz þú illa trúir,
    vildu af hánom þó gott geta:
fagrt skaltu við þann mæla   en flátt hyggja
    ok gjalda lausung við lygi.

46 Þat er enn of þann   er þú illa trúir
    ok þér er grunr at hans geði:
hlæja skaltu við þeim   ok um hug mæla;
    glík skolo gjöld gjöfóm.

47 Ungr var ek forðom,   fór ek einn saman;
    þá varð ek villr vega;
auðigr þóttomz   er ek annan fann:
    maðr er mannz gaman.

48 Mildir, frœknir   menn batst lifa,
    sjaldan sút ala;
en ósnjallr maðr   uggir hotvetna,
    sýtir æ gløggr við gjöfom.

_____

[1] _erost,_ **R**; (cp. str. 32, l. 1).

40 A man should not stint himself in the use of money he has made. Many a time what is meant for friends is being saved up for foes. Things often turn out worse than we anticipate.

41 Friends should rejoice each other's hearts with gifts of weapons and raiment, that is clear from one's own experience. That friendship lasts longest—if there is a chance of its being a success—in which the friends both give and receive gifts.

42 A man ought to be a friend to his friend and repay gift with gift. People should meet smiles with smiles and lies with treachery.

43 A man ought to be a friend to his friend and also to his friend's friend. But no one should be friendly with a friend of his foe.

44 Know—if you have a friend in whom you have sure confidence and wish to make use of him, you ought to exchange ideas and gifts with him and go to see him often.

45 If you have another in whom you have no confidence and yet will make use of him, you ought to address him with fair words but crafty heart and repay treachery with lies.

46 Further, with regard to him in whom you have no confidence and of whose motives you are suspicious, you ought to smile upon him and dissemble your feelings. Gifts ought to be repaid in like coin.

47 I was young once and walked quite alone, and then I went astray. I thought myself a rich man when I found a comrade, for comradeship is the delight of mankind.

48 Generous and bold men have the best time in life and never foster troubles. But the coward is apprehensive of everything, and a miser is always groaning over gifts.

49 Váðir mínar gaf ek velli at
  tveim trémönnum :
 rekkar þat þóttoz er þeir ript höfðo ;
  neiss er nøkkviðr halr.

50 Hrørnar þöll sú er stendr þorpi á,
  hlýrat[1] henni börkr né barr ;
 svá er maðr sá er manngi ann :
  hvat skal hann lengi lifa ?

51 Eldi heitari brennr með illom vinom
  friðr fimm daga ;
 en þá sloknar er inn sétti kømr,
  ok versnar allr vinskapr.

52 Mikit eitt skala manni gefa ;
  opt kaupir sér í lítlo lof :
 með hálfom hleif ok með höllo keri
  fekk ek mér félaga.

53 Lítilla sanda lítilla sæva,
  lítil ero geð guma ;
 því allir men urðot jafnspakir—
  hálf er öld hvar.

54 Meðalsnotr skyli manna hverr,
  æva til snotr sé ;
 þeim er fyrða fegrst at lifa,
  er vel mart vito.

55 Meðalsnotr skyli manna hverr,
  æva til snotr sé ;
 þvíat snotrs mannz hjarta verðr sjaldan glatt—
  ef sá er alsnotr er á.

56 Meðalsnotr skyli manna hverr,
  æva til snotr sé ;
 ørlög sín viti engi fyrir ;
  þeim er sorgalausastr sefi.

---

[1] emend. Rask ; *hlýrar*, **R.**

49 I gave my clothes out in the country to two wooden men. They thought themselves champions when they had the garments: a naked man is ashamed.

50 A young fir-tree withers away when it stands on a mound, neither its bark nor needles protect it. So is it with a man for whom nobody cares—why should he continue to live?

51 Among bad friends affection burns more fiercely than fire for five days, but when the sixth comes it dies out, and all the friendly feeling between them becomes spoilt.

52 It is not necessarily a big gift one ought to give to a man. Esteem is often bought at a small price. With a half loaf and a tilted bottle I have picked up a companion.

53[1] Small are the shallows of small seas, small are the minds of men. All men are not equally wise, for mankind is not always perfect.

54 Every man should be moderately wise, never excessively so. Those people who know a very fair amount have the best time.

55 Every man should be moderately wise, never excessively so. For the heart of a wise man is seldom glad if its owner is a man of very great wisdom.

56 Every man should be moderately wise, never excessively so. He who does not foresee his fate has a mind most free from care.

---

[1] It is hardly possible to give a satisfactory translation of the text as it stands. Cp. note, p. 107.

57 Brandr af brandi   brenn unz brunninn er,
      funi kveykiz af funa :
      maðr af manni   verðr at máli kuðr,
      en til dœlskr af dul.

58 Ár skal rísa   sá[1] er annars vill
      fé eða fjör hafa ;
      sjaldan liggjandi úlfr   lær um getr,
      né sofandi maðr sigr.

59 Ár skal rísa   sá er á yrkendr fá,
      ok ganga síns verka á vit ;
      mart um dvelr   þann er um morgin søfr ;
      hálfr er auðr und hvötom.

60 þurra skíða   ok þakinna næfra,
      þess kann maðr mjöt—
      þess viðar   er vinnaz megi
      mál ok misseri.

61 þveginn ok mettr[2]   ríði maðr þingi at,
      þótt hann sét væddr til vel :
      skúa ok bróka   skammiz engi maðr,
      né hests in heldr,   þótt hann hafit góðan.

62[3] Snapir ok gnapir,   er til sæva kømr,
      örn á aldinn mar :
      svá er maðr   er með mörgom kømr
      ok á formælendr fá.

63 Fregna ok segja   skal fróðra hverr
      sá er vill heitinn horskr ;
      einn vita,   né annarr skal,
      þjóð veit, ef þrír ero[4].

64 Ríki sitt   skyli ráðsnotra hverr
      í hófi hafa :
      þá hann þat finnr,   er með frœknom kømr,
      at engi er einna hvatastr.

---

[1] *Ar skal ri sa er*, **R** ; but cp. str. 59, line 1.
[2] **R** ; *þveginn ok kembðr*, pap. mss.
[3] Written in **R** after 63 but with an indication that the two strophes should be transposed.
[4] emend. Heusler ; *þriro*, **R**.

57 One faggot is set light to by another until it is burnt out, one flame is kindled by another. One man is brought out in conversation by another, but becomes moody through being wrapped up in himself.

58 He ought to get up early who means to take his neighbour's life or property. A wolf in its lair never gets a ham, nor a slumbering man victory.

59 He who has few to work for him ought to get up early and go to see to his work. A man who sleeps during the morning is at a great disadvantage. By the keen man wealth is already half-won.

60 Of dry faggots and shingles for thatching—of such things a man can make an estimate—such timber as will last a quarter or half a year.

61 A man should wash himself and take a meal before riding to court, even if he is not too well clad. No man should be ashamed of his shoes or trousers or of his horse either, though he has not a good one.

62 The eagle coming to the sea hovers with bent head over the hoary deep and snatches at its prey. Not otherwise is it with a man who comes into a throng and has none to speak on his behalf.

63 Every man of learning ought to take part in discussion if he wishes to be reputed wise. (For you know) "Take one into your confidence, but never two; if you confide in three the whole world will know."

64 Every man who is judicious will use his power with moderation. When he mixes with the brave he will discover that no man is peerless in courage.

65 ....
................................;[1]
orða þeira   er maðr öðrom segir,
opt hann gjöld um getr.

66 Mikilsti snemma   kom ek í marga staði,
en til síð í suma ;
öl var drukkit,   sumt var ólagat,
sjaldan hittir leiðr í lið.

67 Hér ok hvar   myndi mér heim of boðit,
ef þyrptak at málungi mat,
eða tvau lær hengi   at ins tryggva vinar,
þars ek hafða eitt etit.

68 Eldr er betstr   með ýta sonom
ok sólar sýn,
heilyndi sitt,   ef maðr hafa náir,
án við löst at lifa.

69 Erat maðr allz vesall,   þótt hann sé illa heill ;
sumr er af sonom sæll,
sumr af frændom,   sumr af fé œrno,
sumr af verkom vel.

70 Betra er lifðom   ok sællifðom[2] :
ey getr kvikr kú ;
eld sá ek upp brenna   auðgom manni fyrir,
en úti var dauðr fyr durom.

71 Haltr ríðr hrossi,   hjörð rekr handarvanr[3],
daufr vegr ok dugir ;
blindr er betri   en brendr sé :
nýtr manngi nás.

72 Sonr er betri   þótt sé síð of alinn
ept genginn guma :
sjaldan bautarsteinar   standa brauto nær,
nema reisi niðr at nið.

---

[1] The lacuna is not indicated in **R.** Cf. note to str. 65 below.
[2] **R** ; *en sé bekkdauðom,* pap. MSS.
[3] emend. Rask ; *hundar-,* **R.**

65 . . . .
A man often pays the penalty for words which he uses
to others.

66 At many a place I have arrived much too early—at others
too late. (Sometimes) the ale had been drunk, at other
times it had not been brewed. An unpopular man rarely
hits on the right moment.

67 Now and then I would be invited to a house when I was
in no need of food for a meal; or two hams would be
hanging up in the house of an intimate friend when I had
already eaten one.

68 The sons of men have no better possession than fire and
sunshine and, if it can be preserved, health combined with
a respectable life.

69 A man is not altogether miserable even if he suffers from
ill-health. One man is blest in his sons, another in his
relations, another in plenty of money, and another in
the success of his undertakings.

70 It is better to be left alive and prosperous. For it is the
living man who always gets the cow. I have seen fire
blazing up ready for a rich man and he was dead outside
the door.

71 The lame can ride a horse, the maimed drive cattle, the
deaf can fight and prevail. It is better to be blind than
to be burnt. A corpse is of no use to anyone.

72 It is well to have a son, though he is born late after the
death of his father. Seldom will memorial stones be seen
by the roadside unless placed there by one relative for
another.

73 Tveir 'ro eins herjar: tunga er höfuðs bani;
     er mér í heðin hvern   handar væni.

74 Nótt verðr feginn   sá er nesti trúir:
     skammar ro skips rár;
     hverf er haustgríma;
     fjölð um viðrir   á fimm dögom,
     en meira á mánaði.

75 Veita hinn   er vetki veit:
     margr verðr af löðrom api;
     maðr er auðigr,   annarr óauðigr,
     skylit þann vítka vár.

76 Deyr fé,   deyja frændr,
     deyr sjálfr it sama;
     en orztírr   deyr aldregi
     hveim er sér góðan getr.

77 Deyr fé,   deyja frændr,
     deyr sjálfr it sama;
     ek veit einn,   at aldri deyr,
     dómr um dauðan hvern.

78 Fullar grindr   sá ek fyr Fitjungs sonom:
     nú bera þeir vánar völ;
     svá er auðr   sem augabragð,
     hann er valtastr vina.

79 Ósnotr maðr,   ef eignaz getr
     fé eða fljóðs munoð,
     metnaðr hánom þróaz,   en manvit aldregi;
     fram gengr hann drjúgt í dul.

80 Þat er þá reynt   er þú at rúnom spyrr,
     inom reginkunnom,
     þeim er gørðo ginnregin
     ok fáði fimbulþulr;
     þá hefir hann batst, ef hann þegir.

81 At kveldi skal dag leyfa,   kono er brend er,
     mæki er reyndr er,   mey er gefin er,
     ís er yfir kømr,   öl er drukkit er.

73 There are two belonging to one company. The tongue is the destroyer of the head. Under every fur coat I expect to find a hand lurking.

74 Night is welcome only to him who is sure of his provisions. Slender are the yards of a ship, and treacherous is an autumn night; weather changes often in five days and still more in a month.

75 He who is ignorant will never know that many a man has been made a fool by vagabonds. One man is wealthy, another poor, but one should not blame him for his misfortune.

76 Cattle die, kinsfolk die, even to us ourselves will death come. But the good fame which a man has won for himself will never die.

77 Cattle die, kinsfolk die, even to us ourselves will death come. One thing I know will never die—the reputation we all leave behind at our death.

78 I have seen the sons of Fitjung with fully stocked folds, now they bear the staff of a beggar. Wealth is like the twinkling of an eye, it is the ficklest of friends.

79 If a foolish man succeeds in getting wealth or the love of a woman, his pride increases but not his common sense; he continues with steadily increasing illusions.

80 Then will be proved what you learn from the runes— those of divine origin which the mighty powers made and the greatest sage engraved: He will do best then if he keeps silent.

81 Praise no day until evening, no wife until she is burnt, no sword until tested, no maid until given in marriage, no ice until crossed, no ale until it has been drunk.

82 Í vindi skal við höggva, veðri á sjó róa,
myrkri við man spjalla : mörg ero dags augo.
Á skip skal skriðar orka, en á skjöld til hlífar,
mæki höggs, en mey til kossa.

83 Við eld skal öl drekka, en á ísi skríða,
magran mar kaupa, en mæki saurgan,
heima hest feita, en hund á búi.

84 Meyjar orðom skyli manngi trúa,
né því er kveðr kona;
því at á hverfanda hvéli vóro þeim hjörto sköpoð,
brigð í brjóst um lagið[1].

85 Brestanda boga, brennanda loga,
gínanda úlfi, galandi kráko,
rýtanda svíni, rótlausom viði,
vaxanda vági, vellanda katli,

86 fljúganda fleini, fallandi báro,
ísi einnættom, ormi hringlegnom,
brúðar beðmálom eða brotno sverði,
bjarnar leiki eða barni konungs,

87 sjúkom kálfi, sjálfráða þræli,
völo vilmæli, val nýfeldom,

88 akri ársánom trúi engi maðr,
né til snemma syni—
veðr ræðr akri, en vit syni,
hætt er þeira hvárt—

89 bróðurbana sínom, þótt á brauto mœti,
húsi hálfbrunno, hesti alskjótom ;
þá er jór ónýtr, ef einn fótr brotnar ;
verðit maðr svá tryggr, at þesso trúi öllo !

90 Svá er friðr kvenna, þeira er flátt hyggja,
sem aki jó óbryddom á ísi hálom,
teitom, tvévetrom, ok sé tamr illa,
eða í byr óðom beiti stjórnlauso,
eða skyli haltr henda hrein í þáfjalli.

[1] emend. Bugge; lagit, **R**.

82 Fell wood in a wind, row out to sea in a breeze, woo a maid in the dark—for many are the eyes of day. Handle a ship so that it glides through the water, use a shield to give protection, a sword to give a blow and a maid to get her kisses.

83 Drink ale by the fire, slide on the ice, buy a horse when it is lanky and a sword when rusty. Feed up the horse at home and the dog in your farm.

84 No one should trust the words of a girl nor what a married woman says; for their hearts have been shaped on a revolving wheel and inconstancy is lodged in their breasts.

85 In a twanging bow,   a blazing fire,
a ravening wolf,   a croaking crow,
a grunting pig,   a rootless tree,
a rising sea,   a boiling kettle,

86 a flying dart,   a falling wave,
ice from one night's frost,   a coiled snake,
a bride's bed talk,   or a broken blade,
a bear's play,   or a king's child,

87 a sick calf,   an independent slave,
the pleasing prophecies of a wise woman,
the corpse of the newly slain,

88 in crops sown early in the year or prematurely in a son no man should place his confidence—weather determines the fate of the crops and intelligence that of the son, and both are uncertain—

89 in your brother's slayer if you meet him on the road, a house half burnt, a horse exceeding swift—the horse is useless if a leg breaks—no man should be so trustful as to trust in any of these.

90 To have the love of women with crafty hearts is like driving on slippery ice with an unroughshod horse (a high-spirited two-year old, not broken in)—or like steering a rudderless boat in a violent wind—or like having to catch a reindeer on thawing hills when you are lame.

91 Bert ek nú mæli,   þvíat ek bæði veit:
    brigðr er karla hugr konom ;
    þá vér fegrst mælom   er vér flást hyggjom :
    þat tælir horska hugi.

92 Fagrt skal mæla   ok fé bjóða
    sá er vill fljóðs ást fá,
    líki leyfa   ins ljósa mans :
    sá fær er frjár.

93 Ástar firna   skyli engi maðr
    annan aldregi :
    opt fá á horskan   er á heimskan né fá
    lostfagrir litir.

94 Eyvitar firna   er maðr annan skal,
    þess er um margan gengr guma ;
    heimska ór horskom[1]   gørir hölða sono
    sá inn mátki munr.

95 Hugr einn þat veit   er býr hjarta nær,
    einn er hann sér um sefa :
    øng er sótt verri   hveim snotrom manni
    en sér øngo at una.

96 Þat ek þá reynda   er ek í reyri sat
    ok vættak míns munar ;
    hold ok hjarta   var mér in horska mær—
    þeygi ek hana at heldr hefik.

97 Billings mey   ek fann beðjom á,
    sólhvíta, sofa :
    jarls ynði   þótti mér ekki vera,
    nema við þat lík at lifa.

98 'Auk nær apni   skaltu, Óðinn, koma,
    ef þú vilt þér mæla man ;
    allt ero ósköp   nema einir viti
    slíkan löst saman.'

99 Aptr ek hvarf   ok unna þóttomz,
    vísom vilja frá ;
    hitt ek hugða,   at ek hafa mynda
    geð hennar allt ok gaman.

---

1 emend. Rask ; *horskan*, **R.**

91 Now I will speak plainly for I have known both. Men are not constant in their love for women. For the falser our hearts the more flattering our words, and so we betray even a clever mind.

92 He who wants to win a woman's love should say flattering things and offer presents—praise the figure of the beautiful maiden. It is the flatterer who is the successful wooer.

93 No man should ever blame another for falling in love. Often a bewitching face will captivate the wise when it has no effect on a fool.

94 A man should in no way blame another for that which is a common weakness. Mighty love turns the sons of men from wise men into fools.

95 The mind alone knows what is near to the heart, and alone is conscious of its feelings. In the opinion of a wise man there is no ailment worse than not to be contented with anything.

96 This I experienced when I sat in the reeds and waited for my love. That wise maiden was body and soul to me; yet I did not win her the more for that.

97 I found the daughter of Billingr asleep on her bed—fair as the sun in her beauty. I felt there could be no possible pleasure for a noble except in living with that fair form.

98 'And towards evening, Óðinn, you ought to come if you intend to woo a maiden for yourself. It will mean utter disgrace if more than two know of such a shameful deed.'

99 Back I turned and thought to enjoy my love in my reckless desire; I believed that I should have complete possession of her mind and love.

100 Svá kom ek næst,　　at in nýta var
　　　vígdrótt öll um vakin,
　　　með brennandom ljósom　　ok bornom viði:
　　　svá var mér vilstígr of vitaðr.

101 Ok nær morni　　er ek var enn um kominn,
　　　þá var saldrótt um sofin;
　　　grey eitt ek þá fann　　innar góðo kono
　　　bundit beðjom á.

102 Mörg er góð mær,　　ef görva kannar,
　　　hugbrigð við hali:
　　　þá ek þat reynda,　　er it ráðspaka
　　　teygða ek á flærðir fljóð;
　　　háðungar hverrar　　leitaði mér it horska man,
　　　ok hafða ek þess vetki[1] vífs.

103 Heima glaðr gumi　　ok við gesti reifr,
　　　sviðr skal um sik vera,
　　　minnigr ok málugr,　　ef hann vill margfróðr vera,
　　　opt skal góðs geta;
　　　fimbulfambi heitir, sá er fátt kann segja:
　　　þat er ósnotrs aðal.

104 Inn aldna jötun ek sótta; nú em ek aptr um kominn;
　　　fátt gat ek þegjandi þar;
　　　mörgom orðom　　mælta ek í minn frama
　　　í Suttungs sölom.

105 Gunnlöð mér um gaf　　gullnom stóli á
　　　drykk ins dýra mjaðar;
　　　ill iðgjöld　　lét ek hana eptir hafa
　　　síns ins heila hugar,
　　　síns ins svára sefa.

106 Rata munn　　létomk rúms um fá
　　　ok um grjót gnaga;
　　　yfir ok undir　　stóðomk jötna vegir,
　　　svá hætta ek höfði til.

　　　　　　　[1] emend. Rask; *vetkis*, **R**.

100 When next I came the bold band of warriors was wide awake and bearing torches of flaming pine. Such was the love-visit in store for me.

101 And when I had come again towards morning the household had fallen asleep, but I found a dog had been tied to the bed of that worthy lady.

102 Many a worthy damsel when you get to know her well shows a heart that is fickle to men. I proved that when I tried to lure that prudent lady into evil ways. The clever maiden sought out for me every humiliation, and none the more did I win the lady.

103 At home a man ought to be cheerful and affable to his guests and self-reliant, but to become a great sage one should cultivate a good memory and eloquent speech and constantly talk of the heroic. Arch-dunce is the name given to the man who can say nothing; that is the characteristic of a noodle.

104 I have just returned from visiting that old Jötunn. Little did I gain by silence there—for it was by many words that I won my suit in the halls of Suttungr.

105 Gunnlöð gave me from her golden throne a drink of the precious mead. It was a poor recompense I made to her for her true feelings and her troubled heart.

106 With the snout of Rati I drilled through the rock and bored a passage for myself. Above and below I was enclosed by rocks—and so I risked my life.

107 Vel keypts litar   hefi ek vel notit—
    fás er fróðom vant—
    þvíat Óðrerir   er nú upp kominn
    á alda vés jarðar.

108 Ifi er mér á   at ek væra enn kominn
    jötna görðom ór,
    ef ek Gunnlaðar ne nytak,   innar góðo kono,
    þeirar er lögðomk arm yfir.

109 Ins hindra dags   gengo hrímþursar
    Háva ráðs at fregna
    Háva höllo í:
    at Bölverki þeir spurðo   ef hann væri með böndom
                              kominn
    eða hefði hánom Suttungr of sóit.

110 Baugeið Óðinn   hygg ek at unnit hafi;
    hvat skal hans tryggðom trúa?
    Suttung svikinn   hann lét sumbli frá
    ok grœtta Gunnlöðo.

111 Mál er at þylja   þular stóli á[1],
    Urðar brunni at;
    sá ek ok þagðak,   sá ek ok hugðak,
    hlýdda ek á manna mál;
    of rúnar heyrða ek dœma,   né um ráðom þögðo,
    Háva höllo at,
    Háva höllo í,
    heyrða ek segja svá:

112 Ráðomk þér, Loddfáfnir,   at þú ráð nemir—
    njóta mundo, ef þú nemr,
    þér muno góð, ef þú getr—:
    nótt þú rísat,   nema á njósn sér
    eða þú leitir þér innan út staðar.

113 Ráðomk þér, Loddfáfnir,   at þú ráð nemir—
    njóta mundo, ef þú nemr,
    þér muno góð, ef þú getr—:
    fjölkunnigri kono   skalattu í faðmi sofa,
    svá at hon lyki þik liðom.

---

[1] *at* written above *á* in a later hand in **R.**

107 I made good use of the beauty so cheaply bought—little is unobtainable by the clever—for Óðrerir has now come up to human habitations.

108 I very much doubt whether I should have come back from the courts of the Jötnar had I not made use of that worthy lady Gunnlöð, whom I took in my arms.

109 The next day the frost-giants went to ask about the state of the High One—in the hall of the High One. They asked whether Bölverkr had returned to the gods or whether Suttungr had slaughtered him.

110 I suppose that Óðinn had sworn a ring-oath. How can his word be trusted? He defrauded Suttungr of his mead and left Gunnlöð in tears.

111 It is time to chant from the seat of the sage, at the well of Fate; I saw and was silent, I saw and pondered, I listened to the speech of men. I heard runes spoken of and the interpretation thereof declared at the hall of the High One; in the hall of the High One, I heard such words as these:

112 I advise you Loddfáfnir to take my advice—you will benefit if you lay it to heart, you will prosper if you accept it—do not rise at night unless you are on the watch or looking for a place outside for yourself.

113 I advise you Loddfáfnir to take my advice—you will benefit if you lay it to heart, you will prosper if you accept it—do not sleep in the arms of a witch or suffer her to take you into her embrace.

114 Hón svá gørir   at þú gáir eigi
þings né þjóðans máls;
mat þú villat   né mannzkis gaman,
ferr þú sorgafullr at sofa.

115 Ráðomk þér, Loddfáfnir,   at þú ráð nemir—
njóta mundo, ef þú nemr,
þér muno góð, ef þú getr—:
annars kono   teygðo þér aldregi
eyrarúno at.

116 Ráðomk þér, Loddfáfnir,   en þú ráð nemir—
njóta mundo, ef þú nemr,
þér muno góð, ef þú getr—:
á fjalli eða firði   ef þik fara tíðir,
fástu at virði vel.

117 Ráðomk þér, Loddfáfnir,   en þú ráð nemir—
njóta mundo, ef þú nemr,
þér muno góð, ef þú getr—:
illan mann   láttu aldregi
óhöpp at þér vita ;
þvíat af illom manni   fær þú aldregi
gjöld ins góða hugar.

118 Ofarla bíta   ek sá einom hal
orð illrar kono :
fláráð tunga   varð hánom at fjörlagi,
ok þeygi um sanna sök.

119 Ráðomk þér, Loddfáfnir,   en þú ráð nemir—
njóta mundo, ef þú nemr,
þér muno góð, ef þú getr—:
veitstu, ef þú vin átt   þannz þú vel trúir,
farðu at finna opt ;
þvíat hrísi vex[1]   ok hávo grasi
vegr er vetki trøðr.

120 Ráðomk þér, Loddfáfnir,   en þú ráð nemir—
njóta mundo, ef þú nemr,
þér muno góð, ef þú getr—:
góðan mann   teygðo þér at gamanrúnom,
ok nem líknargaldr, meðan þú lifir.

¹ vegs, R.

114 She will make you heedless of the court and of the word of the king. You will not wish for food or the joys of mankind, but will go to sleep weighed down with sorrow.

115 I advise you Loddfáfnir to take my advice—you will benefit if you lay it to heart, you will prosper if you accept it—never lure to yourself as confidante the wife of another.

116 I advise you Loddfáfnir and you shall take my advice—you will benefit if you lay it to heart, you will prosper if you accept it—if you desire to journey over mountain or sea, provide yourself with plenty of food.

117 I advise you Loddfáfnir and you shall take my advice—you will benefit if you lay it to heart, you will prosper if you accept it—never let a bad man know of any ill luck which may befall you, for you will never get from a bad man any return for your goodheartedness.

118 I have known a man mortally hurt by the talk of a bad woman—a wily tongue brought about his death, through quite untrue accusations.

119 I advise you Loddfáfnir and you shall take my advice—you will benefit if you lay it to heart, you will prosper if you accept it—know, if you have a friend in whom you have confidence go and see him often, for a path which is never used gets overgrown with bushes and rank grass.

120 I advise you Loddfáfnir and you shall take my advice—you will benefit if you lay it to heart, you will prosper if you accept it—attract to yourself good men in close companionship and you will have a healing charm as long as you live.

121 Ráðomk þér, Loddfáfnir,   en þú ráð nemir—
        njóta mundo, ef þú nemr,
        þér muno góð, ef þú getr—:
     vin þínom   ver þú aldregi
        fyrri at flaumslitom.
     Sorg etr hjarta,   ef þú segja ne náir
        einhverjom allan hug.

122 Ráðomk þér, Loddfáfnir,   en þú ráð nemir—
        njóta mundo, ef þú nemr,
        þér muno góð, ef þú getr—:
     orðom skipta   þú skalt aldregi
        við ósvinna apa;

123 þvíat af illom manni   mundo aldregi
        góðs laun um geta,
     en góðr maðr   mun þik gørva mega
        líknfastan at lofi.

124 Sifjom er þá blandat   hverr er segja ræðr
        einom allan hug;
     allt er betra,   en sé brigðom at vera;
        era sá vinr öðrom, er vilt eitt segir.

125 Ráðomk þér, Loddfáfnir,   en þú ráð nemir—
        njóta mundo, ef þú nemr,
        þér muno góð, ef þú getr—:
     þrimr orðom senna   skalattu þér við verra mann;
        opt inn betri bilar,
        þá er inn verri vegr.

126 Ráðomk þér, Loddfáfnir,   en þú ráð nemir—
        njóta mundo, ef þú nemr,
        þér muno góð, ef þú getr—:
     skósmiðr þú verir   né skeptismiðr,
        nema þú sjálfom þér sér;
     skór er skapaðr illa,   eða skapt sé rangt,
        þá er þér böls beðit.

121 I advise you Loddfáfnir and you shall take my advice—
you will benefit if you lay it to heart, you will prosper if
you accept it—never be the first to break rashly with
a friend. Sorrow will eat out your heart unless you can
tell some one all that is in your mind.

122 I advise you Loddfáfnir and you shall take my advice—
you will benefit if you lay it to heart, you will prosper if
you accept it—you ought never to enter into conversation
with a senseless fool.

123 For you will never get from a bad man any return for
kindness, but a good man will be able to gain for you a
sound and sure reputation.

124 It is a sign of the closest intimacy when a man determines
to reveal his whole soul to someone. There is nothing
worse than to be fickle. He is no friend who never says
anything unpleasant.

125 I advise you Loddfáfnir and you shall take my advice—
you will benefit if you lay it to heart, you will prosper if
you accept it—you should not waste a word in altercation
with a man inferior to yourself; generally, when a worse
man attacks, the better man retires.

126 I advise you Loddfáfnir and you shall take my advice—
you will benefit if you lay it to heart, you will prosper if
you accept it—never be a maker of shoes or shafts except
for yourself alone. If the shoe is misshapen or the shaft
crooked, then a curse will be called down upon you.

127 Ráðomk þér, Loddfáfnir,   en þú ráð nemir—
   njóta mundo, ef þú nemr,
   þér muno góð, ef þú getr—:
   hvars þú böl kant,   kveðu þér bölvi at
   ok gefat þínom fjándom frið.

128 Ráðomk þér, Loddfáfnir,   en þú ráð nemir—
   njóta mundo, ef þú nemr,
   þér muno góð, ef þú getr—:
   illo feginn   verðu aldregi,
   en lát þér at góðo getit.

129 Ráðomk þér, Loddfáfnir,   en þú ráð nemir—
   njóta mundo, ef þú nemr,
   þér muno góð, ef þú getr—:
   upp líta   skalattu í orrosto—
   gjalti glíkir   verða gumna synir—
   síðr þitt um heilli halir.

130 Ráðomk þér, Loddfáfnir,   en þú ráð nemir—
   njóta mundo, ef þú nemr,
   þér muno góð, ef þú getr—:
   ef þú vilt þér góða kono   kveðja at gamanrúnom
   ok fá fögnuð af,
   fögro skaldu heita   ok láta fast vera;
   leiðiz manngi[1] gott, ef getr.

131 Ráðomk þér, Loddfáfnir,   en þú ráð nemir—
   njóta mundo, ef þú nemr,
   þér muno góð, ef þú getr—:
   varan bið ek þik vera,   ok eigi ofvaran;
   ver þú við öl varastr   ok við annars kono
   ok við þat it þriðja,   at þik[2] þjófar né leiki.

132 Ráðomk þér, Loddfáfnir,   en þú ráð nemir—
   njóta mundo, ef þú nemr,
   þér muno góð, ef þú getr—:
   at háði né hlátri   hafðu aldregi
   gest né ganganda.

---

[1] corr. from *margr*, **R**.   [2] add. Rask; omitted in **R**.

127 I advise you Loddfáfnir and you shall take my advice—
you will benefit if you lay it to heart, you will prosper if
you accept it—whenever you notice mischief, regard it as
mischief intended against yourself and give no peace to
your enemies.

128 I advise you Loddfáfnir and you shall take my advice—
you will benefit if you lay it to heart, you will prosper if
you accept it—never rejoice in evil but get your pleasure
out of what is good.

129 I advise you Loddfáfnir and you shall take my advice—
you will benefit if you lay it to heart, you will prosper if
you accept it—look not up in battle—for the sons of men
become mad with terror—lest spells be cast upon you.

130 I advise you Loddfáfnir and you shall take my advice—
you will benefit if you lay it to heart, you will prosper if
you accept it—if you want to persuade a worthy lady to
the closest companionship, and to secure her favour, you
make fair promises to her and let them be binding. No
one is averse to gifts who can get them.

131 I advise you Loddfáfnir and you shall take my advice—
you will benefit if you lay it to heart, you will prosper if
you accept it—I bid you be cautious but not too cautious;
exercise caution most with ale and the wife of another
man, and thirdly see that thieves do not outwit you.

132 I advise you Loddfáfnir and you shall take my advice—
you will benefit if you lay it to heart, you will prosper if
you accept it—never hold a stranger or a traveller up to
ridicule or mockery.

133 Opt vito ógörla   þeir er sitja inni fyrir
hvers þeir ro kyns er koma;
erat maðr svá góðr   at galli ne fylgi,
né svá illr at einugi dugi.

134 Ráðomk þér, Loddfáfnir,   en þú ráð nemir—
njóta mundo, ef þú nemr,
þér muno góð, ef þú getr—:
at három þul   hlæðu aldregi:
opt er gott, þat er gamlir kveða;
opt ór skörpom belg   skilin orð koma,
þeim er hangir með hám,
ok skollir með skrám,
ok váfir með vilmögom.

135 Ráðomk þér, Loddfáfnir,   en þú ráð nemir—
njóta mundo, ef þú nemr,
þér muno góð, ef þú getr—:
gest þú ne geyja   né á grind hrøkkvir[1];
get þú váloðom vel.

136 Ramt er þat tré,   er ríða skal
öllom at upploki;
baug þú gef,   eða þat biðja mun
þér læs hvers á liðo.

137 Ráðomk þér, Loddfáfnir,   en þú ráð nemir—
njóta mundo, ef þú nemr,
þér muno góð, ef þú getr—:
hvars þú öl drekkir,   kjós þú þér jarðar megin;
þvíat jörð tekr við ölðri   en eldr við sóttom,
eik við abbindi,   ax við fjölkyngi,
höll við hýrógi—heiptom skal mána kveðja—
beiti við bitsóttom,   en við bölvi rúnar,
fold skal við flóði taka.

138 Veit ek at ek hekk   vindga meiði á
nætr allar nío,
geiri undaðr   ok gefinn Óðni,
sjálfr sjálfom mér,
á þeim meiði,   er manngi veit
hvers hann af rótom renn.

---

[1] emend. Hildebrand; hrökir, **R**.

133 Those who are present in a house are frequently without information as to the origin of the visitors. There is no man so good as to be free from imperfection or so bad as to be entirely worthless.

134 I advise you Loddfáfnir and you shall take my advice— you will benefit if you lay it to heart, you will prosper if you accept it—never make fun of a grey-haired sage. Often what old men say is sound. Words of wisdom often come from a wrinkled skin—from one who loiters among the hides, and potters about among the skins, and totters about among the drudges.

135 I advise you Loddfáfnir and you shall take my advice— you will benefit if you lay it to heart, you will prosper if you accept it—do not bawl at a stranger nor drive him away from your gate. Show kindness to the poor.

136 It is a strong bolt which has to be raised for all to enter in. Give gifts freely or every kind of plague will be called down upon your limbs.

137 I advise you Loddfáfnir and you shall take my advice— you will benefit if you lay it to heart, you will prosper if you accept it—when you drink ale choose for yourself the might of earth, for earth offers resistance to drunkenness and fire to disease, oak to 'binding,' and an ear of corn to witchcraft, *höll* offers resistance to strife—the moon should be invoked for anger—*beiti* to disease caused by bites and runes to evil. It is the function of land to offer resistance to water.

138 I know that I hung on a windswept tree for nine whole nights, wounded with a spear and given to Óðinn, myself to myself, on a tree about which no one knows from the roots of what (tree) it springs.

139 Við hleifi mik sældo¹   né við hornigi;
      nýsta ek niðr:
      nam ek upp rúnar,   œpandi nam:
      fell ek aptr þaðan².

140 Fimbulljóð nío   nam ek af inom frægja syni
      Bölþors, Bestlo föður,
      ok ek drykk of gat   ins dýra mjaðar,
      ausinn Óðreri.

141 þá nam ek frævaz   ok fróðr vera
      ok vaxa ok vel hafaz;
      orð mér af orði   orz leitaði,
      verk mér af verki   verks leitaði.

142 Rúnar munt þú finna   ok ráðna stafi,
      mjök stóra stafi,
      mjök stinna stafi,
      er fáði fimbulþulr
      ok gørðo ginnregin
      ok reist hroptr rögna,

143 Óðinn með ásom,   en fyr álfom Dáinn,
      Dvalinn³ ok dvergom fyrir,
      Ásviðr⁴ jötnom fyrir;
      ek reist sjálfr sumar.

144 Veitstu, hvé rísta skal?   veitstu, hvé ráða skal?
      veitstu, hvé fá skal?   veitstu, hvé freista skal?
      veitstu, hvé biðja skal?   veitstu, hvé blóta skal?
      veitstu, hvé senda skal?   veitstu, hvé sóa skal?

145 Betra er óbeðit   en sé ofblótit:
      ey sér til gildis gjöf;
      betra er ósent,   en sé ofsóit:
      Svá Ðundr um reist   fyr þjóða rök:
      þar hann upp um reis,   er hann aptr of kom.

---

¹ sældo, E. Magnússon; seldo, R.
² þatan, R.
³ R indicates that the two names 'Dvalinn and Dáinn' should be reversed
in position.
⁴ R; Alsviðr, pap. MSS.

139 They revived me neither with bread nor drink. I peered downwards. I took up the runes, screaming I took them. Thereupon I fell back.

140 Nine mighty spells I learned from the famous son of Bölþorr, Bestla's father, and sprinkled with Óðrerir I got a drink of the precious mead.

141 Then I began to be quickened and full of wisdom, to grow and to thrive. Words coming in succession one after another led me to further words—deeds coming in succession one after another led me to further deeds.

142 You will be able to find the runes and the legible letters, letters of great power and might, which have been painted by the great sage, made by the mighty gods and cut by Óðinn the *hroptr* of the gods among

143 the Aesir, by Dáinn for the elves, by Dvalinn for the dwarfs, by Ásviðr for the giants. I have cut some myself.

144 Do you know how to cut and how to interpret? Do you know how to paint and how to divine? Do you know how to invoke and how to make offerings? Do you know how to sacrifice and how to slaughter?

145 Better there should be no prayer than excessive offering; a gift always looks for a recompense. Better there should be no sacrifice than an excessive slaughter. So Thundr engraved before the history of mankind began. He rose up where he came back.

146 Ljóð ek þau kann   er kannat þjóðans kona
    ok mannzkis mögr;
    Hjálp heitir eitt,   en þat þér hjálpa mun
    við sökom ok sorgom   ok sútom görvöllom.

147 Þat kann ek annat,   er þurfo ýta synir,
    þeir er vilja læknar lifa.

148 Þat kann ek it[1] þriðja: ef mér verðr þörf mikil
    hapts við mína heiptmögo,
    eggiar ek deyfi   minna andskota;
    bítat þeim vápn né velir.

149 Þat kann ek it fjórða: ef mér fyrðar bera
    bönd at boglimom,
    svá ek gel   at ek ganga má;
    sprettr mér af fótom fjöturr,
    en af höndom hapt.

150 Þat kann ek it fimta: ef ek sé af fári skotinn
    flein í fólki vaða,
    flýgra hann svá stint   at ek stöðvigak,
    ef ek hann sjónom of sék.

151 Þat kann ek it sétta: ef mik særir þegn
    á rótom rás viðar,
    ok þann hal   er mik heipta kveðr,
    þann eta mein heldr en mik.

152 Þat kann ek it sjaunda: ef ek sé hávan loga
    sal um sessmögom,
    brennrat svá breitt   at ek hánom bjargigak;
    þann kann ek galdr at gala.

153 Þat kann ek it átta,   er öllom er
    nytsamlikt at nema:
    hvars hatr vex   með hildings sonom,
    þat má ek bœta brátt.

154 Þat kann ek it níunda: ef mik nauðr um stendr,
    at bjarga fari míno á floti,
    vind ek kyrri   vági á
    ok svæfik allan sæ.

[1] *it* omitted in **R.**

146 Such spells I know as are not known to women of royal rank and to the sons of men.
One is called "Help" and it will help you against accusations and sorrows and woes of every kind.

147 A second I know which the sons of men need who wish to be physicians.

148 A third I know: if I am in great need of placing a shackle on my foes, I blunt the blades of my enemies: neither their weapons nor their staves will wound.

149 A fourth I know: if men place gyves upon my arms and legs, I will chant such spells as will set me free— the fetter from my feet shall fly, the shackle from my hands.

150 A fifth I know: if I see a dart maliciously shot whizzing through the host, though its course be unerring I will stay it if my eyes catch sight of it.

151 A sixth I know: if a man wound me by the roots of a sapling, and rather than on myself the hurt will prey on the man who wishes me evil.

152 A seventh I know: if I see a lofty hall blazing above the banqueters, the flames will not spread to such an extent that my help will be unavailing—such a spell I know how to chant.

153 An eighth I know which it is profitable for all to take to heart: should hostility spring up between the sons of a warrior prince I can speedily reconcile them.

154 A ninth I know: if need arises to save my boat on the sea, I can lull the wind over the waves and calm the whole ocean.

155 Þat kann ek it tíunda :   ef ek sé túnriðor
   leika lopti á,
ek svá vinnk,   at þær villar¹ fara
   sinna heim-hama,
   sinna heim-huga.

156 Þat kann ek it ellipta :   ef ek skal til orrosto
   leiða langvini ;
und randir ek gel,   en þeir með ríki fara
   heilir hildar til,
   heilir hildi frá,
   koma þeir heilir hvaðan.

157 Þat kann ek it tólpta   ef ek sé á tré uppi
   váfa virgilná,
svá ek ríst,   ok í rúnom fák,
   at sá gengr gumi
   ok mælir við mik.

158 Þat kann ek it þrettánda :   ef ek skal þegn ungan
   verpa vatni á ;
munat hann falla,   þótt hann í fólk komi ;
   hnígra sá halr fyr hjörom.

159 Þat kann ek it fjórtánda :   ef ek skal fyrða liði
   telja tíva fyrir,
ása ok álfa   ek kann allra skil ;
   fár kann ósnotr svá.

160 Þat kann ek it fimtánda,   er gól Þjóðreyrir
   dvergr fyr Dellings durom :
afl gól hann ásom,   en álfom frama,
   hyggjo Hroptatý.

161 Þat kann ek it sextánda :   ef ek vil ins svinna mans
   hafa geð allt ok gaman,
hugi ek hverfi   hvítarmri kono
   ok sný ek hennar öllom sefa.

¹ emend. Lüning; þᷓ villir, **R**.

155 A tenth I know : if I see phantom riders sporting in the air, I can contrive to make them go bereft of their proper shapes and their proper senses.

156 An eleventh I know: if I have to lead old friends into battle, I chant spells under their shields and they march in their might—safe into the fight—safe out of the fight—from all their conflicts safe they return.

157 A twelfth I know : if I see on a tree aloft a corpse swinging from a halter, I cut and paint runes in such wise that the man walks and talks with me.

158 A thirteenth I know : if I have to sprinkle a young boy with water, he will never fall if he goes into battle—nor will such a man succumb to the sword.

159 A fourteenth I know : if I have to number the gods before a host of men, I have information about all the gods and elves. No one but a wise man has such knowledge.

160 A fifteenth I know which Þjóðreyrir the dwarf chanted before the doors of Dellingr. He chanted strength to the gods, success to the elves, understanding to Hroptatýr.

161 A sixteenth I know : if I wish to have an independent damsel's whole mind and love, I can sway the heart of the white-armed girl and altogether change her affections.

162 Þat kann ek it sjautjánda,   at mik mun seint firraz
it manunga man:—
ljóða þessa   mun ðú, Loddfáfnir,
lengi vanr vera;
þó sé þér góð, ef þú getr,
nýt, ef þú nemr,
þörf, ef þú þiggr.

163 Þat kann ek it áttjánda,   er ek æva kennig
mey né mannz kono—
allt er betra,   er einn um kann;
þat fylgir ljóða lokom—,
nema þeiri einni,   er mik armi verr,
eða min systir sé.

164 Nú ero Háva mál kveðin   Háva höllo í,
allþörf ýta sonom,
óþörf jötna sonom,
Heill, sá er kvað!   Heill, sá er kann!
Njóti, sá er nam!
Heilir, þeirs hlýddo!

162 A seventeenth I know so that the young maiden will be slow to part from me. You will be long in need of these spells, Loddfáfnir. Yet you will prosper if you accept— benefit if you lay them to heart, profit if you receive them.

163 An eighteenth I know which I will never make known to maiden or married woman, save only to her who holds me in her arms, or perchance to my sister. It is always better for only one to know.—And that is the conclusion to my song.

164 Now have the words of the High One been uttered in the hall of the High One—most profitable to the sons of men, but useless to the jötnar. Luck to him who has spoken! Luck to him who has knowledge! May he benefit who has laid these words to heart! Luck to those who have listened!

6 "Sigrúnar þú skalt kunna[1]   ef þú vilt sigr hafa,
   ok rísta á hjalti hjörs,
   sumar á vétrimom,   sumar á valböstom,
   ok nefna tysvar Tý.

7 Ölrúnar skaltu kunna,   ef þú vill annars kvæn
   vélit þik í tryggð, ef þú trúir;
   á horni skal þær rísta   ok á handar baki
   ok merkja á nagli Nauð.

8 Full skal signa,   ok við fári sjá,
   ok verpa lauki í lög:
   þá ek þat veit,   at þér verðr aldri
   meinblandinn mjöðr[2].

9 Bjargrúnar skaltu kunna,   ef þú bjarga vilt,
   ok leysa kind frá konom;
   á lófa þær skal rísta,   ok of liðo spenna,
   ok biðja þá Dísir duga.

10 Brimrúnar skaltu rísta   ef þú vilt borgit hafa
   á sundi seglmörom;
   á stafni skal rísta,   ok á stjórnar blaði,
   ok leggja eld í ár:
   era svá brattr breki   né svá blár unnir,
   þó kømztu heill af hafi.

11 Limrúnar skaltu kunna,   ef þú vilt læknir vera,
   ok kunna sár at sjá;
   á berki skal þær rísta   ok á baðmi viðar
   þeim er lúta austr limar.

12 Málrúnar skaltu kunna,   ef þú vilt at manngi[3] þér
   heiptom gjaldi harm;
   þær um vindr,   þær um vefr,
   þær um setr   allar saman,
   á því þingi   er þjóðir skolo
   í fulla dóma fara.

---

[1] *Völsunga Saga*; *rísta*, **R**.
[2] The last two lines of the strophe are missing in **R** and are inserted from the *Völsunga Saga* xx.
[3] emend. Copenhagen ed. 1787—1828; *magni*, **R**.

THE SIGRDRÍFUMÁL

6 "If you wish to have victory you ought to know *sigrúnar* and cut them on the hilt of your sword, some on the *vétrim* and some on the *valböst,* and utter twice the name Týr.

7 If you do not wish to be betrayed in the confidence you have placed in another's wife, you ought to know *ölrúnar* and cut them on the drinking horn and on the back of the hand, and write *Nauðr* on your nail.

8 You ought to consecrate the cup and take precaution against danger and cast a leek into the liquid. I know that you will then never get mead maliciously prepared.

9 If you wish to relieve a woman and help her to bring forth her child, you ought to know *bjargrúnar* and cut them on the palm of the hand and let them encircle the joints and pray the Dísir for help.

10 If you wish your sailing vessel to be safe on the sea, you ought to cut *brimrúnar,* some on the prow and some on the steering paddle, and place fire to the oar. However big the breakers and however threatening the waves you will come safely off the sea.

11 If you wish to be a doctor and know how to look after wounds, you ought to know *limrúnar,* and cut them on the bark and boughs of a tree whose branches bend to the east.

12 If you wish to prevent anyone from prosecuting a grievance against you with violence, you ought to know *málrúnar.* They are threaded and woven and formed into one compact fabric at meetings where people gather in court.

13 Hugrúnar skaltu kunna,   ef þú vilt hverjom vera
      geðsvinnari guma;
   þær of réð,   þær of reist,
   þær um hugði Hroptr,
      af þeim legi,   er lekit hafði
      ór hausi   Heiðdraupnis
      ok ór horni   Hoddrofnis.

14 Á bjargi stóð   með brimis eggjar,
      hafði sér á höfði hjálm;
   þá mælti Míms höfuð
   fróðlikt it fyrsta orð,
      ok sagði sanna stafi.

15 Á skildi kvað ristnar,   þeim er stendr fyr skínanda goði,
      á eyra Árvakrs   ok á Alsvinnz hófi,
   á því hvéli er snýz   undir reið Hrungnis[1],
      á Sleipnis tönnom   ok á sleða fjötrom,
16 á bjarnar hrammi   ok á Braga tungo,
      á úlfs klóom   ok á arnar nefi,
   á blóðgom vængjom   ok á brúar sporði,
      á lausnar lófa   ok á líknar spori,
17 á gleri ok á gulli   ok á gumna heillom,
      í víni ok í virtri   ok á vilisessi[2],
   á Gungnis oddi   ok á Grana brjósti,
      á nornar nagli   ok á nefi uglo:
18 allar vóro af skafnar,   þær er vóro á ristnar,
      ok hverfðar við inn helga mjöð,
   ok sendar á víða vega;
   þær ro með ásom,   þær ro með álfom,
      sumar með vísom vönom,
      sumar hafa menzkir menn;
19 þat ero bókrúnar,   þat ero bjargrúnar,
      ok allar ölrúnar,
   ok mætar meginrúnar,
      hveim er þær kná óviltar   ok óspiltar
      sér at heillom hafa—
      njóttu, ef þú namt,
      unz rjúfaz regin!

---

[1] emend. Bugge; *Raugnis*, **R**, *Völsunga Saga*.
[2] So *Völsunga Saga*; *ok virtri ok vilisessi*, **R**.

13 If you wish to be a wiser man than anyone else, you ought to know *hugrúnar*. They were read and cut and thought out by Hroptr by means of the liquid which had leaked from Heiðdraupnir's skull and from Hoddrofnir's horn.

14 (He) stood on a cliff with the blade of Brimir; he had a helmet on his head. Then Mímir's head spoke its first wise words and uttered true sayings.

15 (He) said that they had been cut on the shield which stands before the shining god,
on the ear of Árvakr and on the hoof of Alsvinnr,
on the wheel which revolves beneath the chariot of Hrungnir,
on the teeth of Sleipnir and on the straps of a sledge,

16 on the paw of a bear, on the tongue of Bragi,
on the claws of a wolf, and on the beak of an eagle,
on blood-stained wings, and on the end of a bridge,
on the hand of the reliever and the foot of the healer,

17 on glass and gold, and on the talismans of men,
in wine and in newly made beer, and on a favourite seat,
on the spear of Gungnir and on the breast of Grani,
on the nail of a Norn and on the beak of an owl.

18 All those which had been cut were afterwards scraped off and steeped in the holy mead and cast far and wide. Some are among the æsir, some among the elves, some among the wise vanir and some are possessed by human beings.

19 There are *bókrúnar*, there are *bjargrúnar* and all the *ölrúnar* and the glorious *meginrúnar* for anyone who can keep them unfalsified and uncorrupted for his own welfare—benefit (by them) if you have taken them to heart—until the Powers perish.

20 Nú skaltu kjósa   allz þér er kostr um boðinn,
    hvassa vápna hlynr!
    Sögn eða þögn   hafðu þér sjálfr í hug—
    öll ero mein of metin."

21 "Munka ek flœja   þótt mik feigan vitir,
    emka ek með bleyði borinn!
    Ástráð þín   ek vil öll hafa,
    svá lengi sem ek lifi!"

22 "Þat ræð ek þér it fyrsta,   at þú við frændr þína
    vammalaust verir;
    síðr þú hefnir,   þótt þeir sakar gøri;
    þat kveða dauðom duga.

23 Þat ræð ek þér annat,   at þú eið né sverir,
    nema þann er saðr sé:
    grimmar símar   ganga at tryggðrofi,
    armr er vára vargr.

24 Þat ræð ek þér it þriðja,   at þú þingi á
    deilit við heimska hali;
    þvíat ósviðr maðr   lætr opt kveðin
    verri orð en viti.

25 Alt er vant: ef þú við þegir,
    þá þikkir þú   með bleyði borinn
    eða sönno sagðr;
    hættr er heimiskviðr,
    nema sér góðan geti—
    annars dags   láttu hans öndo farit
    ok launa svá lýðom lygi!

26 Þat ræð ek þér it fjórða: ef býr fordæða,
    vammafull, á vegi,
    ganga er betra   en gista sé,
    þótt þik nótt um nemi.

27 Fornjósnar augo   þurfo fira synir,
    hvars skolo reiðir vega:
    opt bölvísar konor   sitja brauto nær
    þær er deyfa sverð ok sefa.

20 Now it is for you to choose since the opportunity is offered you—prince of the sharp sword! It is for you to determine whether I am to speak or be silent. All misfortunes are predestined."

21 "I will not take to flight even if you know I am doomed. I was not born a coward. I will have all your kind advice as long as I live."

22 "First I advise you to conduct yourself blamelessly towards your kinsfolk. You ought not to take vengeance though they give you cause. It is said that this will benefit a man after death.

23 Secondly I advise you not to take an oath unless you mean to keep it: dire Fate attends the breaking of an oath. Wretched is he who violates his plighted word.

24 Thirdly I advise you not to dispute with foolish people in public, for a stupid man often says things that are more harmful than he realises.

25 Any course is difficult: if you do not answer him it will be thought either that you are a born coward or else that you are justly accused; and it is dangerous to be credited with a character which is not a good one, so next day see that his life is put an end to and so pay people out for their lying.

26 Fourthly I advise you—should a wicked witch be living on your route, it will be better to proceed on your journey rather than to be her guest, even though night may overtake you.

27 The sons of men need far-seeing eyes whenever anger impels them to fight. Often malevolent women sit near their path and blunt their swords and senses.

28 Þat ræð ek þér it fimta: þóttu fagrar sér
   brúðir bekkjom á,
   sifjar silfrs¹   láta ðu þínom svefni ráða;
   teygjattu þér at kossi konor!

29 Þat ræð ek þér it sétta: þótt með seggjom fari
   ²ölðrmál til öfug,
   drukkinn deila   skalattu við dólgviðo;
   margan stelr viti vín.

30 Sennor³ ok öl   hefir seggjom verit
   mörgom at móðtrega,
   sumom at bana,   sumom at bölstöfom;
   fjölð er þat er fira tregr.

31 Það ræð ek þér it sjaunda: ef þú sakar deilir
   við hugfulla hali,
   berjaz er betra   en brenna sé
   inni auðstöfom.

32 Þat ræð ek þér it átta,   at þú skalt við illo sjá
   ok firraz flærðarstafi;
   mey þú teygjat   né mannz kono,
   ne eggja ofgamans.

33 Þat ræð ek þér it níunda,   at þú nám bjargir,
   hvars þú á foldo⁴ finnr,
   hvárts ero sóttdauðir,   eða ero sædauðir,
   eða ero vápndauðir verar.

34 Laug⁵ skal gørva   þeim er liðnir ero,
   þvá hendr ok höfuð,
   kemba ok þerra   áðr í kisto fari,
   ok biðja sælan sofa.

35 Þat ræð ek þér it tíunda,   at þú trúir aldri
   várom vargdropa,
   hverstu⁶ ert bróður bani,
   eða hafir þú feldan föður:
   úlfr er í ungom syni,
   þó hann sé gulli gladdr.

¹ emend. Bugge; *sifja silfr*, **R**.
² With this line begins the lacuna in **R**. The following strophes are taken from paper mss (cp. Bugge, *Sæmundar-Edda*, p. 234).
³ emend. Arni Magnússon; *søngur, saungur,* pap. mss.
⁴ emend. Rask; *foldom, foldͦom,* pap. mss.
⁵ emend. Bugge; *Haug,* pap. mss.   ⁶ emend. Bugge; *hvarstu,* pap. mss.

28 Fifthly I advise you, if you see fair women sitting on the benches, do not let the ladies overpower your sleep. Do not lure women to kiss you.

29 Sixthly I advise you—when men exchange drunken and abusive talk—not to contend with an armed man when you are drunk: wine robs many of their wits.

30 Altercation and ale have caused heartfelt sorrow to many men—death to some and calamity to others. There are many things which afflict mankind.

31 Seventhly I advise you—if you find cause for strife with a gallant warrior—it is better for a man of substance to fight than perish in the flames of his house.

32 Eighthly I advise you to beware of evil and avoid faithless dealings. Do not lure a girl or a married woman, nor incite wantonness.

33 Ninthly I advise you to respect corpses wherever you find them unburied—whether the men have died of sickness, by drowning, or by violence.

34 You ought to prepare a bath for those who are dead and wash their hands and head, comb their hair and dry it before they are laid in the coffin, and bid them slumber happily.

35 Tenthly I advise you never to trust the promises of an outlaw's son, if you have slain his brother or laid low his father. There is a wolf in a young son though he be cheered with gold.

36 Sakar ok heiptir   hyggjat svefngar vera,
    né harm in heldr;
    vits ok vápna   vant er jöfri at fá,
    þeim er skal   fremstr með firom.

37 Þat ræð ek þér it ellipta,   at þú við illo sér
    hvern veg at vinom[1].
    Langt líf   þikkjomkak[2] lofðungs vita:
    römm ero róg of risin."

[1] emend. Grundtvig; *vegi*, pap. MSS.
[2] emend. G. Magnússon; *þikkjomzt ek*, pap. MSS.

36 Do not believe that hatred and feuds are lulled to sleep
any more than sorrow. A prince who intends to be first
among men needs to acquire both wisdom and weapons.

37 Eleventhly I advise you to beware in every way of
treachery from friends. I do not think the prince will
have a long life. Mighty is the strife which has been set
on foot.

THE REGINSMÁL

19 "Segðu mér þat, Hnikarr, allz þú hvárttveggja veitst
    goða heill ok guma:
    Hver bötst ero, ef berjaz skal,
    heill at sverða svipon?"

Hnikarr kvað:

20 "Mörg ero góð, ef gumar vissi,
    heill at sverða svipon!
    Dyggva[1] fylgjo hygg ek ins døkkva vera
    at hrottameiði hrafns.

21 Þat er annat: ef þú ert út um kominn
    ok ert á braut búinn,
    tvá þú lítr á tái standa
    hróðrfúsa hali.

22 Þat er it þriðja: ef þú þjóta heyrir
    úlf und asklimom,
    heilla auðit verðr þér af hjálmstöfom[2],
    ef þú sér þá fyrri fara.

23 Øngr skal gumna í gögn vega
    síð skínandi systur Mána:
    þeir sigr hafa er sjá kunno,
    hjörleiks hvatir er þeir hamalt fylkja.

24 Þat er fár mikit, ef þú fœti drepr,
    þars þú at vígi veðr:
    tálar dísir standa þér á tvær hliðar,
    ok vilja þik sáran sjá.

25 Kemðr ok þveginn skal kœnna hverr
    ok at morni mettr,
    þvíat ósýnt er hvar at apni kømr;
    illt er fyr heill at hrapa."

[1] Flat.; *dyggja*, **R.**   [2] Flat.; *hilmstöfom*, **R.**

THE REGINSMÁL

19 "Tell me, Hnikarr, since you know the omens of both gods and men, what are the best omens when swords are flashing if one has to fight?"

20 "There are many good omens when swords are flashing, if men knew them. I think it is lucky for a warrior to have the escort of a black raven.

21 The next is if you are setting out and prepared for a journey and you see two warriors eager for renown standing in your path.

22 A third is if you hear a wolf howling beneath the boughs of an ash tree; if you see them going before you, luck will fall to your lot in encounters with warriors.

23 No man ought to fight facing the last rays of Máni's sister: those shall have victory who can see, bold in fight when they draw up the wedge-shaped column.

24 It is very dangerous to stumble when you go into battle: crafty Dísir stand on either side of you and wish to see you wounded.

25 Every wise man should be combed and washed and have a meal in the morning, for it is uncertain where he will arrive in the evening. It is a bad omen to stumble."

THE GRÓGALDR

5 "Galdra þú mér gal, þá er góðir ero:
  bjarg þú, móðir, megi!
  á vegom allr hygg ek at ek verða muna[1]:
  þikkjomk[2] ek til ungr afi."—

6 "Þann gel ek þér fyrstan, er kveða fjölnýtan
  —þann gól Rindr Rani—:
  at þú af öxl skjótir því er þér atalt[3] þykkir:
  sjálfr leið þú sjálfan þik.

7 Þann gel ek þér annan: ef þú[4] árna skalt
  vilja lauss á vegom,
  Urðar lokkor[5] haldi þér öllom megom,
  er þú á smán sér.

8 Þann gel ek þér inn þriðja: ef þér þjóðáar[6]
  falla[7] at fjörlotom,
  Horn ok Ruðr snúiz til heljar meðan
  ok þverri æ fyr þér.

9 Þann gel ek þér inn fjórða: ef þik fjándr standa,
  görvir á galgvegi[8],
  hugr þeim[9] hverfi til[10] handa þér[11]
  ok snúiz þeim til sátta sefi.

10 Þann gel ek þér inn fimta: ef þér fjöturr verðr[12]
  borinn at boglimom,
  leysigaldr[13] læt ek þér fyr legg of kveðinn,
  ok støkkr þá láss af limom,
  en af fótom fjöturr.

---

[1] *muni*, certain MSS.
[2] *þikkiz ek*, certain MSS.
[3] *atlað*, *ætlað*, certain MSS.
[4] *er þú*, most MSS.
[5] *lokr*, MSS.
[6] ed.; *þjóðar*, *þjoðir*, MSS.
[7] *fara*, certain MSS.
[8] *gaglvegi*, certain MSS.
[9] *hugr þinn*, certain MSS; *hryggvi*, certain MSS.
[10] In most MSS. *til* is missing.
[11] MSS; *þér mætti*, most MSS.
[12] emend. Müllenhoff; *verða*, MSS.
[13] emend. Bugge; *leifnis elda* (*eldir*, *eldo*), *leifinz elða*, MSS.

THE GRÓGALDR

5 "Chant for me spells which will be beneficent. O Mother, help your son! I think that I shall perish on my journeys. I feel that I am too young a man."

6 "A first I will chant to you which is said to be very helpful and which Rindr chanted to Ran—that you may shake off from your elbow what you regard as a source of danger to you. Be your own guide.

7 A second I will chant to you: if you must pursue your quest, without joy on your journey, may the spells of Urðr keep you on every side when you are in a humiliating position.

8 A third I will chant to you: if mighty rivers flow and endanger your life, may Horn and Ruðr be diverted meanwhile to hell and ever recede before you.

9 A fourth I will chant to you: if your enemies stand prepared for you on the path of death, may their hearts be turned to favour you and their minds inclined to reconciliation.

10 A fifth I will sing to you: if fetters are placed on your limbs, I will have a spell chanted to release your legs. The gyves shall fly from your limbs and the fetters from your feet.

11 Þann gel ek þér inn sétta: ef þú á sjó kømr
   meira[1] en menn viti,
   logn ok lögr   gangi þér í lúðr saman,
   ok lé þér æ friðdrjúgrar farar.

12 Þann gel ek þér inn sjaunda: ef þik sœkja kømr[2]
   frost á fjalli há,
   hrævakulði[3]   megit þíno holdi fara,
   ok haldiz[4] æ lík at liðom.

13 Þann gel ek þér inn átta: ef þik úti nemr
   nótt á niflvegi—
   at því firr[5] megit[6]   þér til meins gøra
   kristin dauð kona.

14 Þann gel ek þér inn níunda: ef þú við inn naddgöfga
   orðom skiptir jötun,
   máls ok manvits   sé þér á minni ok hjarta[7]
   gnóga of gefit[8]."

[1] *meir*, certain MSS.
[2] *kynni*, certain MSS.
[3] *hvera kuldi*, one MS.
[4] emend. Bugge; *haldit or*, MSS.
[5] *fyr(r)*, certain MSS.
[6] One MS; *megi at*, most MSS; *megit at*, two MSS.
[7] emend. Detter and Heinzel; *minnis hjarta, mimis hjarta*, MSS.
[8] *getit*, most MSS.

11 A sixth I will chant to you : if you are going on a sea mightier than any that men know, may tranquil waters fall to your lot and a calm journey ever be granted you.

12 A seventh I will chant to you : if frost overtake you on a lofty mountain, may the chill of death not have power to injure your flesh and may your body ever keep the use of its limbs.

13 An eighth I will chant to you—if night overtake you out on the misty road, that so a dead Christian woman may have less power to bring you misfortune.

14 A ninth I will chant to you : if you enter into conversation with the giant with the magnificent spear, may speech and wisdom be granted to you in abundance in your memory and heart."

NOTES

THE HÁVAMÁL

1. *þvíat...á fleti*, lit. 'for it is uncertain in what house enemies are present.' For Óðinn's own experiences as a stranger in the house of another, see the *Vafþrúðnismál*. This strophe is quoted by Snorri in *Gylf*. II. Cp. also *Árkiv f. nord. Filol*. 1902, p. 72.

2. *á bröndom.* Paper MSS read *á brautom*, a reading which Munch has adopted. Rask reads (in accordance with one paper MS) *at bröndom*, i.e. 'at the fireside.' The prep. *á* is difficult to explain. Various other interpretations have been suggested; Fritzner, s.v. 'posts erected on both sides of the entrance to a house'; Ólsen (*Arkiv*, 1893, p. 223) 'on the fire-wood'; Magnússon (*Camb. Philol. Soc. Proc.* 1884, pp. 29 ff.) 'on snow shoes'; Egilsson (s.v.) 'in extremest need.' Attention should perhaps be drawn here to the similarity between this passage and the opening strophes of the *Vafþrúðnismál* in which Óðinn as the stranger insists on speaking *á golfi* until he has proved his learning. The *golf* was the central space in the hall and it was here that the fire was made (cp. *Rígsþula* 2, 14, *Egils Saga* LV etc.). It seems to me therefore that, in spite of the (perhaps archaic) use of *á* (with which we may compare *Beow.* l. 926) editors have been too hasty in rejecting the old interpretation, especially in view of the fact that the next strophe begins with *elz*. The fireside was the natural place for a stranger to approach when craving hospitality. We may compare the *Odyssey* VII. 153 ff., where it is said of Odysseus on his arrival at the palace of Alcinous:

'Ὡς εἰπὼν κατ' ἄρ' ἕζετ' ἐπ' ἐσχάρῃ ἐν κονίῃσιν
πὰρ πυρί.

freista frama, cp. *Vaf.* 11. Magnússon translates 'try his luck.'

3. In *Vaf.* 8 Óðinn himself is a traveller requiring hospitality.

4. Cp. *Vaf.* 8.

þjóðlöð and *endrðaga* are ἀπ. λεγ. Some editors associate the latter with *þiggja* (Magnússon, *Camb. Philol. Soc. Proc.* 1887, p. 8), others connect with *þegja* as on p. 45, in which case the lit. transl. would be 'silence in turn,' i.e. while the guest himself is speaking. Cp. Ólsen, *Arkiv*, 1914, p. 52.

góðs um œðis...orz, lit. 'a word of good feeling,' i.e. showing kindly feeling (F. Jónsson). Bugge and Gering emend to *orð* and punctuate *góðs um œðis ef sér mætti orð*, i.e. 'if (the host) is to gain for himself a reputation for good feeling.'

5. *dælt er heima hvat.* Heusler includes this phrase in the list of proverbs inserted in the *Hávamál* (*Zeitschrift d. Vereins für Volkskunde*, 1915, 1916, p. 110).

at augabragði, cp. str. 30.

6. l. 4, cp. *Málsháttakvæði* 22, l. 87: *sjaldan hygg-ek at gyggi vörom.* l. 5, cp. *Vaf.* 10, *Beow.* l. 1059 and Proverbs xiv. 15.

7. *þunno hljóði.* Egilsson notes *s.v. þunnr* the Icelandic expression: *þunt er móður eyrað.*

8. Cp. Magnússon's comments (*Camb. Philol. Soc. Proc.* 1887, pp. 10 f.).

10. Here as in str. 26, 30, 31 and *Sigr.* 25 the MS has *þikk-* (for *þykk-*).

11. *velli at.* In the *Háv.* str. 38, 49 *völlr* would seem to mean the country, away from one's home, perhaps originally forest lands separating one inhabited district from another.

13. Cp. the first riddle in the *Hervarar Saga* XI *hann stelr geði guma*. In the *Sigrdrífumál* 29 the same phrase occurs. Cp. also *Háv.* 131.

14. This Fjalarr seems to be identical with the Suttungr of str. 104 and 110. In *Skaldskaparmál* I he is one of the dwarfs who betray Kvasir. The name also occurs in the *Völuspá* 16 for a dwarf, in str. 42 for a cock, and in the *Hárbarzljóð* 26 for a giant.

16. Cp. Saxo, p. 259, 'His final fate carries off every living man: doom is not to be averted by skulking.'

17. Cp. str. 13 and note. *kópir. ἀπ. λεγ.* This word is preserved in mod. Norw. dialects. *uppi er þá geð guma.* F. Jónsson: 'it is all over with him,' cp. however the proverb : 'What soberness conceals, drunkenness reveals.'

18. This sentiment recurs constantly in Norse Literature. *viða ratar.* Cp. the description of Kvasir, *Bragarœður* I. *fjölð um farit.* Cp. *Vaf.* 3 passim.

19. Cp. *Vaf.* 10.

21. *mál.* The MS reading may possibly be right. Parallels for the gen. after negatives (as in Slav.) are given by Bugge, *Edda*, p. 394.

22. *ok illa skapi.* A curious construction ; one would have expected *illu skapi* or *illa í skapi*; cp. *Laxdœla Saga* LXXXIV. *era vamma vanr.* Cp. *Lok.* 30.

24—27. The parallelism in the construction of these strophes should be noted. Cp. Phillpotts, *Elder Edda*, p. 94.

24. *þótt...sitr*, lit. 'if he is sitting among sensible people, though they show' etc.

26. *í vá.* Egilsson (s.v.) translates 'danger'; some editors translate 'corner' and compare *Sigurðarkviða en skamma* 29 (*vá* for *vrá*); Fritzner translates 'home' and compares place-names in *-voom*.

27. Cp. *Grettis S.* XCI: *Engi er allheimskr er þegja má* ; and Proverbs xvii. 28 'Even a fool when he holdeth his peace is counted wise.'

28. *gengr um guma.* This idiom occurs twice in the *Hávamál*—here and in str. 94—and three times in Skaldic poetry. In each case it seems to mean 'that which overpowers a man,' in the *Hávamál* apparently his human weaknesses.

29. *staðlauso. ἀπ. λεγ.* *nema haldendr eigi*, lit. 'unless restrainers possess it.' *ógott um gelr.* Cp. *Lok.* 31.

30. Cp. str. 132 for a similar sentiment. *at augabragði.* Derision was forbidden by law and punished by outlawry (*Grágás* I. CVI.).

31. *glissir, glami.* In mod. Norw. dialects these words mean respectively 'to titter' and 'to make a noise of merry making.'

32. *gagnhollir. ἀπ. λεγ.* The word may however mean 'thoroughly good-natured.' *rekaz.* The earlier form *vrek-* is required for the alliteration. Cp. *Sigrdr.* 27. *þat.* Possibly however *þat* should be taken with what goes before.

33. *snópir* occurs also in *Gautreks Saga* 13 (a verse) and is preserved in mod. Norw. dialects and mod. Icelandic. In Norw. it means 'to make a champing noise when eating.' In mod. Icel. it is preserved with the meaning 'to waste one's time.' For the related *snapa*, cp. *Háv.* 62.

sólginn. Cp. *Haust.* 16 and the compound *brim-sólginn.*
For the sentiment of the first two lines compare *Reg.* 25.
Ólsen (*Arkiv,* 1914, p. 54) accepts Bugge's emendation of *nema* to *nei án.*

34. Cp. A.-S. *Exeter Gnomic Verses,* l. 146, *oft mon fereð feor bī tune þǣr him wāt frēond unwiotodne.*

35. Cp. *Egils Saga* LXXVIII; and *Grettis Saga* XXXIV. Apparently a proverb common to several countries; there is a Slavonic saying: 'A guest and fish smell the third day.' Cp. the *Laws of Canute,* II. 28.

36. Alliteration fails in line 1 of **R.** Bugge emends to *búkot.* Cp. Ólsen (*Arkiv,* 1914, p. 59) for a discussion of the matter.
halr er heima hverr. Cp. for a similar expression *Málsháttakvæði* 16. 5. Heusler, *Zeitschr. des Vereins für Volksk.* 1915, p. 111, cites the Gaelic proverb 'a man is king in his own house.'
taugreptan. Cp. *taug,* 'rope' (A.-S. *teag*). If we compare also *Grímnismál* 9: *sköptum's rann rept,* we should perhaps translate 'thatched (or roofed) with fibre'; we may however refer to *vanda-hús* and translate 'house built with twigs' (Saga of St Ólaf XXIII). Cp. V. Guðmundsson, *Privatboligen,* pp. 114 ff.; and R. Meringer, *Etymol. zum geflochtenen Haus* (Halle, 1898).
For references to such houses cp. *Encyc. Brit.* p. 290, under 'Scandinavian Civilisation,' and G. W. Schulz-Minden, 1913, 'Das germ. Haus' (*Mannus Bibl.* 1914).

37. The alliteration of line 1 fails as in str. 36.

38. We may note the difficulty in Iceland of attempting to check lawlessness on the part of the upper classes. In Norway the government had no doubt somewhat more control, though it was probably not very effective in early times. Cp. *Hákonarmál* 17.

39. Line 3 is defective in **R.** The paper MS reading is *svági örvan;* Munch inserts *gjöflan;* F. Jónsson suggests *glǫggvan* by analogy with str. 48. The two former insertions would mean the repetition in the last two lines of the strophe of the meaning of the first two lines. F. Jónsson's *glǫggvan* introduces a new idea into the latter half of the strophe—that a miser does not desire a present lest he should have to give one in return.
at ei...þegit. For the meaning of *þegit* compare the similar use of the participle in str. 60 and 143; lit. 'that accepting was not acceptable (to him).' So Gering. Perhaps, however, we should translate (with Egilsson) 'that accepting (from him) was not (regarded by him as something) accepted' (i.e. a debt).
at leið...ef þegi, cp. str. 130. For the form *þegi* (for *þiggi*) cp. Noreen³, § 488, Anm. 7.

41. *þat...sýnst.* Or should this be taken with the following line as in str. 32? In that case l. 4 is perhaps to be taken with l. 1.
viðrg., endrg., lit. those who exchange and requite gifts.

42. Cp. Hesiod, *Works and Days:* 'Love him that loveth thee and visit him that visiteth thee. To the giver one giveth but none giveth to him that giveth not. A gift is good.' (Transl. A. W. Mair, Oxford, 1908, p. 13.) We may compare also the *Exeter Gnomic Verses,* l. 145. Heusler suggests that line 2 is a proverb.

44. *veitstu.* Cp. a similar use in str. 119, *Sonatorrek* 8, and in *Lokasenna* 4.

46. *ok um hug mæla.* Cp. *Atlamál* 74.

48. Line 4 may mean either 'over receiving' or 'over giving' gifts.

49. *trémönnum.* The singular *trémaðr* elsewhere appears to mean a 'wooden man.' It is used in *Flat.* I. 403 for the two wooden men who were said to have been buried with the god Freyr and afterwards taken out of the barrow and worshipped. In *Ragnars S.* XXI certain men find a very large *trémaðr* in a wood in Samsey. When they enquire about the idol it begins to speak in verse. It is a remarkable fact that the verses show a certain resemblance to the *Háv.* 49 and 50.

Str. 1, l. 4,   *þá varð ek þessa*   *þorps ráðandi.*
Str. 3,   *þar báðu standa*   *meðan strönd þolir,*
           mann hjá þyrni   *ok mosavaxinn;*
           nú skýtr á mik   *skýja gráti*
           hlýr hvárki mér   *hold né klæði.*

The first strophe occurs again in an almost identical form in *Halfs Saga* II, where it is said to come from a voice in the barrow of the king called *Ögvaldr* (cp. *Ólafs Saga Trygg.*, Heimskringla LXXI). The point of giving clothes to two idols is not obvious, though the idol in the verses in the *Ragnars Saga* complains that it is unprotected by 'flesh and clothes.' For possible remains of such a figure (upon an altar) cp. S. Müller, *Nord. Altertumskunde*, II. pp. 179 f.

50. The meaning of the word *þorp* here is obscure, as it is also unfortunately in the only other passage in the Edda where it occurs (*Vaf.* 49). In prose the word means 'a hamlet or village'—which does not seem to be appropriate here. The meaning 'field' suggested by Vigfusson would be in accordance with the Gothic *þaurp* (ἀγρός), a ἅπ. λεγ. in Nehemiah v. 16. Egilsson proposes 'cairn,' which would suit the passage in *Halfs Saga* II very well. Others have suggested 'heap' as a Norwegian dialectal meaning. Could the meaning of *þorp* here be so explained?

The thought of loneliness seems to quicken the imagination of the Edda poets as much as anything. We may compare with this simile *Hamðismál* 5:

       Einstæð em ek orðin   *sem ösp í holti,*
       fallin at frændom   *sem fura at kvisti,*
       vaðin at vilia   *sem vitr at laufi.*

53. The first two lines of this strophe have always proved a crux and none of the solutions proposed can be regarded as satisfactory. For various suggestions as to its probable meaning, cp. Fritzner, III. 264; Vigfusson, p. 393; Egilsson, sub *lítill.* Ólsen (*Arkiv*, 1914, p. 64) would emend to *litlir eru sandar lítilla sæva.* Is it possible that *lítilla* (in both cases or in the first only) should be read as *lítil lá*? The translation would then be: 'small are the breakers (surf) made by shores and seas,' or 'small is the surf of the shores of small seas.'

því...jafnspakir. F. Jónsson omits *því*; most editors emend to *þvíat* with Hildebrand, but this hardly makes the connection more clear. May not *því* be used, like *þat* in str. 32, 46, 148 etc., to introduce a new clause: 'for this reason...namely that'?

hálf er öld hvar. This phrase is also obscure.

hálf. By analogy with a similar use in *Gulaþingslög* 266 Detter and Heinzel suggest the translation, 'divided into two parts'; Egilsson however would translate 'imperfect, incomplete.' It might perhaps be taken more literally, like our phrase 'only half there,' i.e. 'half endowed in some cases.'

hvar. Detter and Heinzel take *hvar* as equivalent to *hvarvetna* everywhere; so Egilsson, Gering etc.; Bugge would read *hvár.*

54. Some editors hold that the phrase *vel mart* must mean 'a very great deal' in accordance with later usage. To give sequence of thought with the first part of the strophe, they suggest the emendation *er* to *era*. The policy of moderation advocated in str. 54 to 56 is one of the radical principles of the *Hávamál* philosophy.

56. *örlög...sefi,* lit. 'no-one should have knowledge beforehand of his fate; his mind (i.e. the mind of him who has no such knowledge) is most free from care.'

58. Cp. *Vápnfirðinga Saga* XIII, where the last two lines of this strophe are quoted as a proverb. Cp. also Saxo, p. 191.

59. *hálfr...hvötom* may however be translated : 'Half a man's wealth depends on his energy' (Gering). Cp. *Egils Saga* I : *var þat síðr hans at rísa upp árdegis ok ganga þá um sýslur manna eða þar er smiðir vóru ok sjá yfir fénað sinn ok akra.*

60. *þakinna.* For a similar use of the participle, cp. note on str. 142. Egilsson takes *þak-* as an adj., and compares *þaknæfrar, N. G. L.* II. 138.

R reads *þess kann maþr mjotuðc*—the last three letters deleted. Cp. the use of *mjöt* in the *Höfuðlausn* 20.

61. Cp. *Reg.* 25 for similar advice.

62. *snapir.* This word only occurs here and in *Lokasenna* 44. It is preserved with the same meaning in mod. Icelandic.

gnapir. Cp. *Brot af Sigurðarkviða* 7. A similar nature picture is indicated in the *Völuspá.* We may compare also the Icelandic *Physiologus (Aarböger,* 1889, XIV.). What is the likeness the poet wishes to emphasize—an attitude of dejection suggested by *gnapir*—or a snatching (at protection) perhaps suggested by *snapir?* The latter seems to be more likely, but the analogy is not clear.

svá er maðr...fá. Cp. str. 25.

63. It would seem, if the strophe is to be coherent, that the last two lines may be a proverb inserted without explanation but implying some such introductory phrase as 'for you know.' The proverb will not then be applied in its usual sense, as it would be an argument for publicity instead of secrecy. Cp. *Málsháttakvæði* 9. Heusler (*Zeitschr. des Vereins für Volksk.* 1915, p. 113) quotes the Norwegian *dat tvo veit, dat veit alle.*

64. Cp. *Fáf.* 17.

65. The first two lines of the strophe are missing in **R** (though no lacuna is marked) but are supplied as follows in some paper MSS :

> gætinn ok geyminn skyli gumna hverr
> ok varr at vintrausti.

Translate : 'Every man should be guarded and discreet and slow to trust even a friend.'

66. *mikilsti* for *mikilstil.* Cp. *helzti* for *helzt til.*

ólagat. ἅπ. λεγ. Egilsson compares *laga* (from *lögr*), i.e. 'to pour out into a vessel' (specially used of malt).

lið. Most editors so interpret the reading *lid* of **R** ; Ólsen (*Arkiv,* 1914, p. 67) reads *lið* and translates 'ale.' For different explanations of *lið* see Falk, *Arkiv,* v. 112; F. Jónsson, *Arkiv,* XIV. 202 (and Egilsson, s.v. *liðr* 1).

68. *án......lífa*, lit. 'without living in dishonour.' Egilsson s.v. *án* suggests the emendation *ok án löst at lífa*, 'and to live without shame.'

70. Many editors emend *ok sællifðom* to *en sé ólifðom* with Rask by analogy with *Fáf.* 31. They would translate: 'It is better to possess life than to be without it.' For the metre cp. Gering, *Die Rhythmik des Ljódhaháttr*, Halle, 1902, p. 218.

ey getr kvikr kú. Cp. *Málsháttakvæði*, strophe 4, line 7 and the Danish proverb *Queger mand faar vel ko, men död faar aldrig liv.* Can this proverb have originated in the ancient custom of paying wergelds in cows? The last two lines of the strophe would allow of several explanations. They may contain a reference to cremation (cp. Egilsson s.v. *fyr* B, 3); or to the hearth fire (Detter and Heinzel). Line 4 may complete the reference to cremation in l. 3, or it may point a contrast between the warmth within and the presence outside of a dead body, whether that of the rich man himself, or of someone else—or possibly the abstract 'death' itself may be meant. The first interpretation would seem to imply that the pyre was lighted before the dead man was placed on it; but was this the case?

71. A clear reference to cremation, and it is noteworthy that this appears to be the normal method of disposing of the dead. Cp. also str. 81.

72. *bautarsteinar.* This form only occurs here. We find however in the *Fagrskinna* 34, *bautaðar steinn*, and in the *Heimskringla, bautasteinar.* Cp. preface to the *Ynglinga S.*: *Hin fyrsta öld er kölluð brunaöld, þá skyldi brenna alla dauða menn ok reisa eptir bautasteina.* And cap. VIII: *en eptir alla þá menn er nökkut mannsmót var at, skyldi reisa bautasteina.*

Various suggestions have been made as to the meaning of the word; Vigfusson compares *brautar kuml*, i.e. *monumentum viæ* (on the inscriptions themselves); Fritzner suggests that *bauta* is a modification of *bautaðar* (? obelisk) or is the genitive form of *baut* (dialect 'a blow,' cp. *sverðbautinn*); Egilsson suggests that it may come from *baut* (f.) (a grave). According to *Hávamál* it would seem as if these stones were arranged along the sides of the road as the Romans placed theirs on the roads outside the city. A good series of pictures of such monuments is to be found in Du Chaillu, I. cap. xviii.

73. The connection of this strophe with the context is not clear to me. Heusler (*Zeitschrift des Vereins für Volkskunde*, 1915, p. 114) suggests that it is composed of three proverbs, which have been inserted to inculcate distrust. He compares *tveir' ro eins herjar* with the med. Latin: *duo sunt exercitus uni* (i.e. *zweie sind dem einzelnen eine Übermacht*), and with the Danish *To ere een Mands Herre.* For *tunga er höfuðs bani*, cp. O. Swed. *tunga huwdhbani liggi i ugildum akri* (transl. *Die Zunge (sein) Haupttöter er liege unbüssbar*). The phrase however may mean that one's own talk might bring about one's own death. Cp. also Ólsen (*Arkiv*, 1914, pp. 73 ff.). He points out that *eins herjar* is a v.l. in *Vaf.* 41.

74. This strophe again seems to consist of proverbs, the connection of which with the context is not clear to me. The first lines seem to mean that only a man who is well furnished with provisions (cp. str. 116) can look forward with equanimity to the prospect of being held up by uncertain weather.

skammar ro skips rár. This line (apparently another proverb, cp. the *Málsháttakvæði* 12. 1) has been frequently discussed; cp. Ólsen, *Arkiv*, 1914, 77 f. and Heusler, *Zeitschrift des Vereins für Volkskunde*, 1915, p. 115. I do not feel sure however that the right explanation has yet been discovered.

haustgríma. Cp. *Alvíssmál* 30: 'It is called night among men...the mighty powers call it *gríma*'; cp. also the phrase *myrkvar grímur*, *Hervarar S.* IV.

75. R reads *margr verðr af loðrom api*, which fails in alliteration. Rask emends to *af öðrom* (cp. G. Jónsson); Grundtvig, *af aurom*; Hildebrand, *auði um* (by analogy with the *Sólarljóð* 34). F. Magnusen compares the Danish proverb: *En Abe kommer andre til at glo og gabe; en Nar gjør flere.* I do not think the true reading has yet been found.

loðrom. Cp. *löþrmenni*, *Fornaldar S.* III. 437.

vítka. I have translated according to Egilsson (s.v.) who suggests that this is a verb only occurring here from *víti.* Some editors emend to *vætkis vaa* (with Grundtvig, *Sæmundar-Edda* (1874)).

76 and 77. The first part of these two strophes is quoted in the *Hákonarmál*, str. 21. Cp. also *The Wanderer*, l. 109.

78. The name Fitjung would seem to have originated from *fita* (fat) (cp. *fitja*, 'to bind up with ointment'). Cp. *Odyssey*, XXIV. 304 f.

80. *Þat er þá reynt.* This passage might also mean 'This will be proved when....'

reynt. Does the word mean 'prove true'?

reginkunnom. This phrase occurs elsewhere only in an inscription on a stone at Fyrunga, *rûnô fâhî raginakundo* (Brate, *Arkiv*, x (N. F.), 331); Fritzner and Gering translate 'of divine origin'; Vigfusson, 'world known.'

ginnregin. Cp. *Hymiskviða* 4, *mærir tívar ok ginnregin* and in such compounds as *ginn-heilög.* Egilsson suggests that the word may be an epithet for the Vanir.

fimbulþulr. Cp. Introduction, p. 10. *Fimbul* occurs in only five compounds, three of which are peculiar to the *Hávamál.* In *Grímnismál* 27, *fimbulþulr* occurs as the name of one of the rivers flowing throughout the universe. In all cases it seems to mean 'mighty, great.'

This strophe should perhaps be read in connection with *Háv.* 111 and *Sigrdr.* 13–18, where the ritual of such ceremonies is elaborated. There is clearly a similarity in phrasing between this strophe and 142, though the general tone of this section of the poem is very dissimilar to that of str. 142 ff.

81. For the change of metre, cp. Introduction, p. 4. For the sentiment, cp. the doctrine of Solon, Herodotus, I. 32.

82. *veðri á sjó róa*, i.e. 'good weather.' Cp. a strophe attributed to Thjóðólfr of Hvín quoted in *Haralds S. Hárf.* XXXVII. This meaning .is more common in Anglo-Saxon. Cp. *Exeter Gnomic Verses* 77.

83. *en hund á búi.* This phrase would seem to be explained by the expressions *búigriðungr* and *heimagriðungr* (*Þorsteins þáttr hvíta* IX).

magran mar kaupa. Cp. *Málsháttakvæði* 21 and Ólsen, *Arkiv*, 1914, p. 80.

84. The last two lines of the strophe occur also in *Fóstbræðra S.* VII.

hverfanda hvéli. An epithet given to the moon in *Alvíssmál* 14. In *Grettis S.* XLII we find the phrase *þvíat mér þykkir á hverfanda hjöli mjök um hans hagi,* where it seems to mean 'inconstant, fickle,' as here. The origin of the phrase has been variously explained as due to (1) the wheels of a carriage (Lüning); (2) the wheel of Fortune (Fritzner) as in *F. M. S.* I. 104; (3) the potter's wheel (Gering).

85. *brestanda boga.* Cp. *Saga of Ólaf Tryggvason, F. M. S.* I. 182. *rótlausom viði.* Can this mean 'a gallows-tree'? Cp. the 'rootless tree' in the Shetland Song (note to str. 138).

86. *beðmálom.* ἀπ. λεγ.

87. *völo vilmæli.* The völur were wise women who were thought to have supernatural power and the gift of prophecy. References to them are frequent both in Norse poetry and prose; for a detailed description cp. *Thorfinns S. Karlsefnis* III.

In the Stockholm pap. MS of 1684 (based on the **R** text of the *Hávamál*) we find inserted after *val nýfeldom*:

> heiðríkum himni,   hlæjanda herra
> hunda helti   ok harmi skœkju
>   óðmála manni,
>   dýri í svelti.

Cp. note by Bugge, *Sæmundar-Edda,* p. 53. This may be translated: 'a clear sky, a laughing lord, the lameness of dogs (? a lame dog), and the grief of a harlot, a man's excited talking, a starving animal.'

88. A parenthesis.

89. The list of untrustworthy things is continued from str. 87; all are in the dative case in apposition with *þesso öllo* which is governed by *trúi.*
verðit...öllo. Cp. Shakespeare, *Lear* III. 20: 'He is mad that trusts in the tameness of a wolf, a horse's health or a whore's oath.'

90. *óbryddom.* Lit. 'without frost-nails.' In a letter to Ólsen, 1911, K. J. Sunström states that these 'frost-nails' have been found in Viking graves and are preserved in museums. In appearance they would seem to be like human shoes (rather than horse shoes) with one spike on the under surface, and they were tied to the horses' hoofs by straps. They are very similar to the frost-nails worn by men in Iceland, called in modern times *mannbroddar* (cp. *Vápnfirðinga S.* III). Such frost-nails were used also for cattle. See *Arkiv,* 1915, p. 80.

94. Cp. *C. P. B.* I. 213: *munaðar riki hefir margan tregat.*
um margan gengr guma. Cp. str. 28. There is apparently a redundant use of the particle *er* in line 1 of the strophe. Gering, gloss. s.v. *er* I. A, 1.

95. *einn er hann sér.* With Egilsson (s.v. *of* A, 12) I take *sér* as pron. refl. Gering, Detter and Heinzel etc. interpret as 3 sing. of *séa (sjá).*
hveim snotrom manni may be dependent on *sótt verri* (i.e. 'no worse ailment for a wise man').

96–101. These strophes describe an adventure of Óðinn with the daughter of Billingr. The story is not to be found elsewhere in Norse literature, but the name Billingr occurs in *Völuspá* 13 (H.) as that of a dwarf, and in a dirge by Ormr Steinþorsson occurs a kenning *Billings á burar full* (cp. *C. P. B.* II. p. 322 and the note in vol. I. p. 463). The name Billing also occurs in *Widsið,* l. 25—the name of a ruler of the Warni— and is common in Anglo-Saxon place-names.
Some such adventure as this may be vaguely hinted at in the Anglo-Saxon poem *Deor,* ll. 14 ff.

96. *í reyri.* The word *reyrr* only occurs here in the Edda. Elsewhere it occurs either in kennings or in compounds. Editors cite this as evidence of the Norwegian origin of the poem.

100. *með......viði,* perhaps a hendiadys. I have taken this passage as an allusion to the use of torchlight processions at marriage ceremonies.

vilstígr, so the MS. Many editors emend to *vílstígr* perhaps by analogy with *margan vílstíg varð hann at ganga, Saga Sverris Konungs* XVIII (*F. M. S.* VIII), but the irony implied in the MS reading is perhaps more consonant with the general tone of the passage.

101. Cp. Saxo, pp. 363 ff. Ragnar, who is wooing Ladgerda, finds a dog and a bear awaiting him in the porch, put there by the maiden to thwart her would-be lover.

102. The MS reading is defended by Bugge. Cp. str. 21, note.

103. This strophe seems to form an introduction to the next episode in the poem, Óðinn's adventure with Gunnlöð.

málugr forms the link with str. 104 for it was by *mörgom orðom* that Óðinn was successful with Gunnlöð. Othello's wooing of Desdemona offers an interesting parallel, cp. Shakespeare, *Othello,* I. 3. 128 ff.

góðs geta, i.e. 'to make mention of.' For this use of *geta,* cp. Fritzner (s.v.); Egilsson suggests as a translation for the whole phrase 'discuss some shining example.'

fimbulfambi occurs only here; *fimbul-* is obsolete except in five compounds, in each of which it has intensifying force. Three of these compounds occur in the *Hávamál* (str. 80, 103, 142). *-fambi,* cp. s.-w. Lincolnshire dial. (Skinner, 1671), 'he fambles so in his talk' (Wright's *Dialect Dictionary, famble,* i.e. 'to stutter'; cp. Danish *famle*).

104–110. These strophes relate Óðinn's experiences when acquiring the poetic mead, cp. Introduction, p. 31. For details of the story reference should be made to the *Bragarœður, Skald.* I. There are points of resemblance between this story and that in Saxo, pp. 94 ff., in which Óðinn's discreditable adventure with Rinda, the daughter of the King of the Ruthenians, is recounted. On the possible connection between this episode and the *Hávamál* strophes, 96–101, 104–110, compare the Introduction, p. 33.

105. *svára.* An antithesis is possibly intended with *heila,* lit. 'sound,' 'healthy.'

106. Rati, the auger (cp. *Bragarœður, Skald.* I.).

jötna vegir, lit. 'roads of the *Jötnar,*' a kenning for 'rocks.'

107. *vel keypts litar.* Fritzner translates 'beauty purchased at a fair price.' Vigfusson and Powell and others read *vél* ('by craft'); F. Jónsson emends to *hlutar.* But cp. the expression *gott (góð) kaup.*

á alda vés jarðar. The MS reading is preserved by Rask, who translates *populorum habitationis terrae.* For the form *jarðar* (acc. pl.) see Noreen, § 381, Anm. 2. Bugge emends *jarðar* to *jaðar* and suggests that the phrase stands for *Miðgarðr;* F. Jónsson emends to *alda vé* (for *vé alda*) *jaðars,* i.e. Óðinn's abode—a phrase describing Valhalla.

109. *Bölverki.* Cp. the part he plays in *Bragarœður, Skald.* I.

sóa occurs also in strophe 144, where it seems to mean sacrificial slaying as in *Ynglingatal* 9.

Háva, apparently a title for Óðinn; cp. also str. 109, 111, and 164, and the title of the poem.

110. *Baugeið.* Cp. *Eyrbyggja S.* IV, *Atlakviða* 30, *Sax. Chron.* 876 etc.

sumbli. Cp. *Alvíssmál* 33 and 34. 'What is the name of that ale...? The sons of Suttungr call it *sumbl.*' Note the impersonal reference to Óðinn here. The rest of the story is told in the first person.

111–137. A series of strophes which by their gnomic character are to be compared with the first part of the poem. The form of the strophes however is different, for with five exceptions each is introduced with a set formula—*Ráðomk þér*, etc. Gnomic verses with a similar literary framework, i.e. *þat ræð ek þér it fyrsta*, are to be found in *Sigrdr.* 22 ff. In pap. MSS this series of strophes is called *Loddfáfnismál.* For a discussion of this strophe, cp. Introd. pp. 8 ff.

111. *þylja.* The word is here used in a ritual sense; we may contrast its use in str. 17.

Urðar brunni at. Cp. *Völuspá* 19, where it is placed under Yggdrasil's ash; according to the *Gylfaginning* XV it was there that the gods held their tribunal every day.

manna mál. Many editors emend to *Hávamál* with Müllenhoff; F. Jónsson suggests that *manna* may stand for gods (cp. *Vegtamskviða* 14); Mogk considers that the epithet refers exclusively to the *Loddfáfnismál*; Miss Phillpotts would emphasize the plural number and suggests that it may indicate that there was more than one speaker.

For a consideration of this strophe and its relationship to the following strophes, cp. Introduction, pp. 38 ff.

112. *Loddfáfnir.* The meaning of this name is obscure; cp. Introd. p. 10, footnote 1.

ráðomk. This form is probably 1 sing. of either the Present Indicative or Present Subjunctive of the verb *ráða*—middle or passive. For examples of the use of such 1 sing. forms with active meaning, cp. Noreen³, § 521, note 2; § 524, note 3.

For other explanations of this form, cp. J. Thorkelsson, *Arkiv*, VIII. 36, and Bugge, *Studier*, I. 327.

njóta mundo etc., better 'you will benefit if you take it, you will prosper by it if you adopt it.'

ráð, lit. 'counsels' (pl.).

þú leitir...staðar. Cp. *Ynglinga S.* XIV.

113. *fjölkunnigri...liðom.* Cp. the story of Harold the Fairhaired and the daughter of the Finn Svasi, *Haralds S. Hárf.* XXV; cp. also *Sigrdr.* 26.

114. Fritzner emends *þjóðans máls* to *þjóðar máls* (cp. *Arkiv*, I. 22 ff.). Compare the description in the *Grípisspá* 29:

> Hón firrir þik   flesto gamni,
> fögr áliti   fóstra Heimis;
> svefn þú ne søfr,   né um sakar dœmir,
> gáraðu manna,   nema þú mey séir.

115. *eyrarúno at*, i.e. 'as mistress'; cp. *Völuspá* 39; we may refer to the *Sigrdr.* 28 and 32 for similar advice.

117. *gjöld ins góða hugar* may perhaps mean 'rewarded by his kind thought'; *Grímnismál* 3 however offers an analogy to the translation adopted above which is that of Vigfusson and Powell. (Cp. Gering.)

118. *Reginsmál* 3 and 4 give the penalty for such an offence.

C. H.   8

119. Cp. str. 44.

120. *gamanrúnom,* 'intimacy in (lit. mysteries of) social pleasures.' Cp. *Háv.* 130 (and *Sigrdr.* 5, where the meaning seems to be somewhat different).

121. *flaumslitom.* ἅπ. λεγ. I have followed Detter and Heinzel. Other editors take *flaum-* here as 'friendship.'

122. *api,* lit. 'ape,' hence perhaps 'fool.' This meaning seems to suit *Háv.* 75 and *Grímnismál* 34 ; the only other occasion on which the word occurs in the Edda is in the obscure passage in *Fáf.* 11.

123. *af illom manni.* Is this a suggestion that foolishness and evil are synonymous ? Cp. *illz mannz kveð' ek aldrei verða grandalausar gjafir, Gautreks S.* I.
líknfastan at lofi. The phrase will allow of various interpretations. Detter and Heinzel suggest 'liked and esteemed.' Perhaps also 'safely established in reputation,' or 'to preserve and secure your reputation.'

124. *allt er betra....* For parallel constr., cp. Detter and Heinzel, p. 132. Cp. Faroese proverb, *vinur er ið' vomm sær* (Hammershaimb, no. 211).

125. Cp. *Háv.* 122 and *Sigrdr.* 24.

126. *skósmiðr, skeptismiðr.* ἅπ. λεγ. Cp. *Arinbjarnar Drapa,* str. 19, *né auð-skept almanna spjör.*

127. *ok gefat þínom fjándom.* Cp. *Helgakv. Hjör.* 34.
þér. Cp. Ólsen, *Arkiv,* 1914, p. 84. R has Þ, which may stand for either *þér* or *þat.*

128. *lát þér at góðo getit.* Cp. *Flateyjarbók* I. 289, 15, and *Grettis Saga* 149²³.

129. *gjalti* (from *geilt,* an Irish loan word). It only occurs here in poetry, but is frequent in prose in the phrase *verða at gjalti* ; cp. *Eyrbyggja S.* XVIII. Originally the word had no connection with O.N. *göltr* (dat. *gelti*), 'a boar,' but later through confusion it was used as a dative of this word and became synonymous in meaning with *svíngalinn* ; cp. Fritzner (s.v.). Kuno Meyer states that this effect of battle on men is a very common feature in Irish story. We may compare also the incident described by Saxo, p. 274, *gjalti glíkir,* lit. 'like frenzy.'
heilli halir. Cp. *Sigrdr.* 27. In the *Ynglinga S.* VI. the power is ascribed to Óðinn himself.
þitt. Detter and Heinzel take the possessive here as equivalent to the pers. pron. Cp. also Egilsson s.v. *heilla.*

130. *at gamanrúnom.* Cp. *hnigom at rúnom, Guðrúnarkviða* III. 4. Cp. also 120 above.
láta fast vera may mean however 'constantly repeat them.'
manngi is the scribe's emendation of an original *margr.* If we preserve *margr* we should translate : 'everyone gets tired of a good thing if he can get it.'

133. One of the paper MSS has the following lines inserted after *koma*—

> Löstu ok kosti   bera ljóða synir
> blandna brjóstum í.

Translate : 'The sons of men carry both vice and virtue mingled in their breasts.' See Bugge, *Edda,* p. 59.

134. *hangir með hám.* Aasen gives dialect meaning of *hangar*, 'to remain idle'; cp. too *Heilagra Manna S.* II. 367. 6.
há occurs in mod. Icelandic compounds—*hrosshá, nautshá.*
váfir. Cp. the use of the word in *Egils S.* LXXXV. verse 1.
vilmögom. In *Skírnismál* 35 it seems to mean 'underlings.' In *Egils S.* LXXXV. a similar picture is given of Egil as an old man.
E. Magnússon, with whom some editors agree, interprets these lines otherwise (*Camb. Philol. Soc. Proc.* 1887). He translates *vilmögom* (dative of *vilmagi*) the 'intestinal maw,' and would translate the whole passage 'hangs among the hides, swings among the skins and rocks among the rennets.'

135. *né á grind hrøkkvir,* lit. 'nor drive him to the (outer) gate'; Jónsson and others read *hrekir*; for the meaning of *grind,* cp. *Gylfaginning* XLIX. Paper MSS insert *þeir mun líku þér lesa,* i.e. 'they will bless you.'

136. *ramt* etc. This strophe is generally interpreted as meaning that one must be hospitable even if the door is worn out with continual opening. The precise meaning of *tré* is uncertain. See Detter and Heinzel, note *ad loc.*
l. 3. *þat,* apparently ref. to *öllom.* Cp. str. 49.
For an example of the open hospitality advocated here, compare the description of Geirriðr, *Eyrbyggja S.* VIII.
Ólsen (*Arkiv*, 1914, p. 85) understands *tré* as 'club.' The meaning would then be: It is a mighty club which has to be swung against all who try to enter.

137. This strophe consists of a series of magical receipts—some of which are obscure. Cp. Cederschiöld (*Arkiv*, 1910, p. 295) and Ólsen (*Arkiv*, 1914, p. 89) where modern parallels are cited. Many parallels may be found in the Anglo-Saxon Leechdoms.
þvíat jörð...ölðri. Most editors refer to the drink given by Grímhildr to Guðrún and compounded according to *Völsunga Saga* XXII of *jarðar magni ok sæ.* The Edda MS *Guð.* II. 2 however reads *urðar magni.* In *Hyndluljóð* 43 we find that Heimdallr was *aukinn jarðar megni.*
tekr við, 'resists,' according to Fritzner, 3. v. 3; 'receives' according to Egilsson.
abbindi. ἅπ. λεγ. Cp. Egilsson s.v.
ax við fjölkyngi. This reference is obscure. The phrase *ax óskorit* in the *Guðrúnarkviða* II. 22 does not appear to throw light on the matter.
hýrógi. ἅπ. λεγ. By analogy with the preceding phrases the MS reading should apparently be translated: 'the hall resists strife in the household,' but the meaning is not clear. Cp. Egilsson (s.v.). Vigfusson emends to *hýrógr við haul* and translates 'spurred rye...against hernia.' Ólsen (*op. cit.*) suggests that *höl* may mean 'elder tree' (Dan. *hyll*).
heiptom...kveðja. The text does not make clear whether the invocation is for protection against the anger of another or for quelling one's own anger.
beiti við bitsóttom. *Bitsóttom* also occurs in *Ynglingatal* 24 where we are told that a king Eysteinn died of this disease; Egilsson suggests a disease due to the bites of insects or snakes.
beiti. Vigfusson would translate 'heather' (cp. *beitilyng*); other editors identify with *beit,* i.e. 'pasturage': Cederschiöld (*Arkiv*, 1910, p. 298) suggests 'alum'; Ólsen, 'beet' (Lat. *beta*), a plant mentioned by Pliny as effective against bites.

skal in l. 9 is functional, as in str. 82, l. 3 and frequently in the Anglo-Saxon Gnomic Verses, esp. Cott. l. 50 ff.

The general similarity between the vocabulary of this strophe and that of *Guðrúnarkviða* II. 21–23 is to be observed.

138–145. These strophes give an obscure account of the acquisition of the Runes by Óðinn. F. Jónsson attributes this obscurity to the fact that they are fragments from different poems—a suggestion supported by the irregularity of the metre and of the strophic form. For a more detailed consideration of the subject-matter, cp. Introduction, p. 35. In the paper MSS this section is given the title *Rúnatals þáttr Óðins.*

138. *veit.* This word is written with a large initial letter in the MS and at the beginning of a fresh line.

ek hekk. Or perhaps 'I have hung.'

vindga meiði may also be translated 'wind-tossed gallows.' Bugge and Egilsson etc. take *vindga* to be the dative singular of *vindugr* (cp. *vargtré vindkald, Hamðismál* 17). A similar phrase *vinga meiði* (with the meaning 'gallows') appears in *Egils S.* LV—which may have been taken from the *Hávamál.* The phrase *vingameiðr* (nominative singular) in the *Háleygjatal* 7 is more difficult to explain in connection with the *Hávamál* phrase as it points either to a compound word or to *vinga* as a genitive.

nætr allar nío, no doubt 'days' as usual in early Teutonic languages. For prominence given to the number nine, cp. Egilsson s.v. *níu.*

geiri undaðr. Cp. *Gautreks S.* VII. We may compare the marking of Óðinn himself, *Ynglinga S.* X.

sjálfr is inserted over a mark of omission.

hvers...renn. Cp. *Fjölsvinnsmál* 20, where the phrase *af hverjom rótom renn* is used of the *Mímameiðr.*

Karl Blind believed that he had found a parallel to this strophe in the following, sung by an old woman on the Shetland Islands—a suggestion which Bugge comments on in his *Studier,* I. 309 ff.

> Nine days he hang pa de rütless tree,
> For ill wis da folk in' güd wis he.
> A blüdy mæt wis in his side,
> Made wi' a lance, 'at wid na hide.
> Nine lang nichts i' da nippin rime
> Hang he dare wi' his næked limb.
> Some dey leuch,
> Bitt idders gret.

139. I have adopted Magnússon's reading *sældo* (from *sæla,* i.e. 'to make happy'). Bugge (*Studier,* I. 345) suggests *sældo* from *sœla* ('to slake'). Vigfusson preserves the MS reading and takes *seldo* as the preterite tense of *selja,* 'to give.' Cp. also Detter and Heinzel, *ad loc.*

fell ek aptr. The meaning of this phrase is obscure but apparently it should be read in close connection with the last line of strophe 145. Detter and Heinzel explain 'I fell again down and returned to my former condition.' Cp. also F. Jónsson, *Arkiv,* 1898, 203. The same expression occurs in *Sigurðarkviða en skamma* 23.

þaðan. This word may be used of time, place or reason. Ólsen suggests that its original place in the strophe was after *niðr* and that it has now taken the place of an original *ofan* (*Arkiv,* 1914, p. 94). Note that alliteration is wanting.

140. The Copenhagen edition emends *Bölþors* to *Bölþorns*, thus identifying Bestla with that Bestla who was the daughter of the giant Bölþorn and the mother of Óðinn, Vili, and Vé. Of her brother nothing is known; Rydberg suggested that he was Mímir. *Fimbulljóð.* Cp. *Háv.* 80, note.

ausinn Óðreri. Is *ausinn* in the nominative or the accusative case? The former (with the meaning 'sprinkled with') would refer to Óðinn, the latter (with the meaning 'drawn up from') to *Óðrerir*, the drink. *Óðreri.* The word only occurs twice in the Poetic Edda, *Háv.* 107 and 140; cp. also however the Prose Edda, *Skaldskaparmál* I. The association of a drink with wisdom and the acquisition of wisdom by means of suffering are to be found in the *Völuspá* 28, 29. The opening stanzas of the *Jómsvikingadrápa* refer to the belief that Óðinn acquired the gift of song from beneath the gallows.

141. For the construction *orð af orði* etc., cp. *Háv.* 57. The first two lines are similar to the expressions used for the growth of a child in the *Rigsðula* 9 and 22; here however it seems to refer to mental growth.

142. *ráðna stafi.* Cp. Runic inscription on the stone at Holm *runar ek rist auk rapna staue.* For a similar use of the participle, cp. *Háv.* 60. *er fáði fimbulþulr ok gørðo ginnregin.* Cp. str. 80 and note. *ginnregin.* Cp. Egilsson s.v. *hroptr rögna,* i.e. Óðinn. Cp. *Sigrdr.* 13 and Egilsson (s.v.).

143. *Dáinn* is the name of a dwarf in *Völuspá* 11 (H), and *Hynd-luljóð* 7. *Dvalinn,* the name of a dwarf. Cp. *Alvíssmál* 16, *Völuspá* 11, 14, *Hervarar S.* II etc. *Ásviðr.* Not known elsewhere.

144. This strophe seems to suggest by means of questions the ritual attendant on magic practices. *hvé ráða skal.* Cp. *Atlamál* 11. *hvé senda skal.* Cp. Falk, *Arkiv,* v. (N. F. I), 111 f.

145. *ey sér til gildis gjöf.* Clearly a proverb, cp. *Háttatal* 26. The connection between this strophe and the general argument, as well as between the various clauses in the strophe itself, is not clear. In the last line there is possibly a reference to str. 139. *Þundr.* Cp. *Grímnismál* 54, where this is a name of Óðinn.

146. *þjóðans kona.* Cp. *Egils Saga* XXXVII, where it is said of Gunnhildr the wife of Eric Blood-Axe: *Gunnhildr var allra kvenna vænst ok vitrust ok fjölkunnig mjök.* We may compare too such people as Sigrdrífa, Grímhildr and Brynhildr.

147. Although this strophe appears to be incomplete, there is no indication of a lacuna in **R.** *lifa,* lit. 'live as.' The sentence might also mean 'whom the physicians wish to survive'; but cp. *Sigrdr.* 11. For other series of charms in which each strophe is introduced by the formula, *þat kann ek...* we may compare *Sigrdr.* 22 ff. and *Gróg.* 6 ff. A similar formula is found on the long Runic inscription at Rök—*þat sagum an(n)art...þat sagum tvælfta...* etc.

148. *bítat þeim...né velir.* Cp. *Ynglinga S.* VI which is perhaps taken from the *Hávamál.* This power was claimed not only by Óðinn himself but by others skilled in magic; cp. *Sigrdr.* 27. In the *Hamðismál* the sons of Jónakr are immune from wounds by weapons and therefore stones are hurled at them in battle.

heiptmögr. ἁπ. λεγ.

149. Cp. *Gróg.* 10, and Bede, IV. 22: *an forte litteras solutorias, de qualibus fabulæ ferunt, apud se haberet, propter quas ligari non posset.*

150. *flýgra...stöðvigak.* Lit. 'it will not fly with such impetus that I will not stop it if....'

151. **R** has *sera.* Does this stand for *særa,* 'to wound,' or for *sœra,* 'to conjure,' i.e. call down imprecations upon? That such conjuring took place we know from *Grettis S.* LXXXI : "Afterwards she took her knife and cut runes on the root and reddened them in her blood, and said spells over them...."

rás viðar. Cp. *Skirnismál* 32, where Skirnir threatens to go *til hrás viðar* to get the *gambantein.*

For *rár*: *hrár* cp. *C. P. B.* II. 572 ; Detter and Heinzel, note *ad loc.* ; Ólsen, *Arkiv,* 1914, p. 94.

heipta kveðr. I have followed Egilsson, Gering, etc. Vigfusson gives 'lay imprecations on (me)' which seems to suit the context better.

152. The first line of the strophe has defective alliteration as it stands; but cp. Ólsen, *Arkiv,* 1914, pp. 94 f. Gering emends *hávan* to *sviþinn.*

In *Ynglinga S.* VII Óðinn is said to be endowed with this power—*með orðum einum at sløkkva eld.* In the *Rígsðula* 44, Konr who was skilled in runes was able to quell fires.

153. *hildings sonom* may be a kenning for 'princes' (cp. its frequent use in this sense in the Helgi Poems).

bœta, lit. 'repair it.'

154. *vind ek kyrri.* Cp. *Gróg.* 11, and *Sigrdr.* 10.

In *Rígsðula* 44, Konr is represented as being able to calm the sea.

155. The MS reading *villir* has been emended to the feminine form *villar* to conform with the feminine *túnriðor.* See however *Arkiv,* 1916, pp. 76 ff., 83 ff.

túnriðor. ἁπ. λεγ. Cp. however similar compounds, *myrkriður, kveldriður, trollriður.* For a vivid account of such night riding we may compare the story of Geirríðr and Gunnlaugr related in the *Eyrbyggja S.* XVI. In *Eyrbyggja S.* XXXIV we find also allusion to the belief that the ghosts of the dead were thought to ride the roofs.

heim hama...heim huga, apparently compounds. Egilsson interprets *hamr* as that skin which remains behind at home while the witch casts her skin and goes forth into the air in a foreign shape. In the *Ynglinga S.* VII, Óðinn is described as having this power. A similar belief is recorded by R. H. Nassau, in *Fetichism in W. Africa,* pp. 326 ff.—A wife is discovered by her husband to attend witch-revels. She leaves her body behind her and assumes the shape of 'three things.' Her husband prevents her return by smearing the inanimate body with pepper and the wife, unable to assume her proper shape, hides in a wood pile and is destroyed.

In *Egils S.* LVII a similar spell is cast on the *land-vættir*—*svá at allar fari þær villar vega.*

156. *und randir ek gel.* Cp. the custom mentioned by Tacitus, *Germania,* III.

157. *virgilná.* ἁπ. λεγ. This power is ascribed to Óðinn also in the *Ynglinga S.* VIII; cp. also *Vegtamskviða* 4.

158. *verpa vatni á.* References to this custom are common in Norse literature; cp. Du Chaillu, II. cap. III.

160. R reads *Þjóðreyrir.* The name does not occur elsewhere in the Edda. The alliteration in the preceding and following strophes perhaps points to '*f*' as the initial letter of this word.

fyr Dellings durom. Dellingr was the father of Day; cp. *Vafþruðnismál* 25; hence this phrase may have meant 'at sunrise.' The conception implied here has been very widely held throughout the world. We may compare modern (e.g. Hausa) folk-tales in which extraordinary things happen at the gates of the dawn. For the use of this phrase as a refrain, cp. Heiðrek's *Riddles, Hervarar S.* XI. *Hroptatý.* Cp. *Grímnismál* 54, and the term *hroptr rögna* (*Háv.* 142).

161. *hafa geð allt ok gaman.* Cp. *Hárbarzljóð* 18.

162. For the significance of the mention of Loddfáfnir in this strophe, cp. Introduction, p. 9.

THE SIGRDRÍFUMÁL

Sigrdrífa has been awakened by Sigurðr from her magic sleep. For the preceding strophe see p. 42. Sigrdrífa is the speaker except in str. 21.

6. *Sigrúnar,* lit. 'victory runes.'

vétrimom, meaning obscure; perhaps part. pl. for sing., as also *valböstom.* Some editors understand the central ridge to be meant. Cp. Falk, *Altnordische Waffenkunde,* 28.

valböstom, meaning obscure. Cp. *Helgakviða Hjörvarðssonar* 9, *en á valbösto verpr naðr hala,* apparently a reference to damascening. Cp. Du Chaillu, I. p. 231.

Týr—god of battle. Cp. *Gylfag.* xxv.

In *Grípisspá* 17, Grípir describes the wisdom which Sigurðr will learn from Sigrdrífa: 'She will teach you, O powerful one, all those runes which men have wished to know.'

7. *Ölrúnar.* It is clear from the strophe that in its present form the word *ölrúnar* means 'ale runes' (cp. also strophes 5 and 8), though this may not have been its original meaning. (Cp. *alu,* an unexplained word often found in the earliest runic inscriptions.)

á horni. Cp. the drinking horn described in *Guðrúnarkviða* II. 22. *Nauðr,* the name of the letter *N* in the runic alphabet. Cp. p. 42, note 3.

8. *lauki.* Egilsson: 'for flavouring and also as a poison-destroying remedy.' Kennings show that it was used as an ingredient in ale. *meinblandinn mjöðr.* Cp. *Lok.* 3.

9. *Bjargrúnar,* i.e. 'relieving runes.'

Dísir. Cp. *Reginsmál* 24 (note). The word would seem to mean here *nornir*; cp. *Fáfnismál* 12: 'Who are the nornir who are midwives and help mothers to give birth to their children?' Cp. also *Oddrúnargrátr* 7 and 8 where Oddrún chants spells over Borgný which cause her to bring forth her child:

> ríkt gól Oddrún,   ramt gól Oddrún,
>   bitra galdra at Borgnýjo.

It is very probable that in *Fjölsvinnsmál* 22 we find other magical remedies for women in travail.

10. *Brimrúnar,* i.e. 'sea runes.' Cp. *Háv.* 154, *Ynglinga S.* VII and *Gróg.* XI.

seglmörom, lit. 'sail-horses' (possibly pl. for sing.); cp. A.-S. *brimhengest,* etc.

leggja eld í ár, lit. 'put fire to the oar.' Egilsson suggests 'magic.' Could *eldr* mean a runic symbol used for magic purposes? Vigfusson interprets *leggja eld,* 'to brand.'

stjórnar blaði. Cp. Frontispiece, Du Chaillu, I.

11. *Limrúnar,* i.e. 'bough runes.' Cp. *Egils S.* LXXII f. *baðmi.* Cp. Vigfusson s.v. (but 'stock' *C. P. B.).* Egilsson, Gering, etc. read *barri* with *Völs. S.*

12. *Málrúnar,* lit. 'speech runes.' Cp. *Guðrúnarkviða* I. 23. A figurative interpretation of the weaving metaphor would seem to be more probable, though the preceding and following strophes require to be taken literally. In the *Atharva-Veda* VI, ii, 27 there is a section giving charms for securing influence in the assembly, etc. : 'Charms against opponents in debate, undertaken with the pâtâ plant. May the enemy not win the debate. Thou art mighty and overpowering. Overcome the debate of those that debate against us; render them devoid of force, O plant.' Transl. Bloomfield, *Sacred Books of the East,* Vol. XLII, p. 137.

13. *Hugrúnar,* lit. 'mind runes.'

Hroptr, i.e. Óðinn. Cp. *Völuspá* 62, *Grímnismál* 8, *Lokasenna* 45, *Háv.* 142, 160 (see notes). The word occurs also in compounds.

Heiðdraupnis. This name is not mentioned elsewhere in Norse poetry.

horni Hoddrofnis. In *Gylfaginning* XXXIX Eikþyrnir's horns are said to exude water into Hvergelmir. We may compare the story of Amalthea and the horn of plenty.

14. *Á bjargi...eggjar.* The subject of the verb *stóð* is not indicated. Bugge suggests that *brimis* is the genitive of a proper name and compares *Grímnismál* 44 ; cp. also Egilsson (s.v.).

Míms höfuð. Cp. *Völuspá* 46 : *mælir Óðinn við Míms höfuð,* and *Ynglinga S.* IV : 'Óðinn had with him Mímir's head which gave him tidings of other regions.' In the *Gylfaginning* we are told that at the *ragnar røk* Óðinn will ride to Mímir's well to take counsel of Mímir for himself and his host. For a modern parallel reference may be made to Dr Haddon's *Head Hunters,* p. 91 (London, 1901). Writing of their customs in Murray Island he says—'the modelled and decorated skulls...were kept mainly for divinatory purposes.'

15. *Á skildi...goði.* Cp. *Grímnismál* 38 :

> *Svalinn heitir,*   *hann stendr sólo fyrir,*
>   *skjöldr, skinanda goði.*

á eyra Árvakrs. One of the steeds of the sun ; cp. *Grímnismál* 37. This phrase is missing from the *Völsunga S.* version.

á Alsvinns hófi, the other steed of the sun (*Grímnismál* 37). *Völsunga S.* reads *Alsvins höfði.*

á því hvéli...Hrungnis. Cp. Bugge's note, *Sæmundar-Edda,* p. 230.

á Sleipnis tönnom. Óðinn's eight-legged steed.

16. *á Braga tungo.* Cp. *Gylfaginning* XXVI.

á brúar sporði. Is this Bifröst? The epithet occurs elsewhere in prose but not in verse.

á lausnar lófa, etc. Cp. str. 9. The meaning would seem to be 'the hand of the midwife and the foot of the doctor,' lit. 'the palm of relieving and the footprint of healing.'

17. *í víni ok í virtri.* Cp. the phrase *virtur og so vin* of the Faroese Ballads.

á Gungnis oddi. There are no other references to this spear in the Poetic Edda though Snorri says that Óðinn had it with him in the *ragnar rǫk* (*Gylfaginning* LI); in the *Skáldskaparmál* XXXV Gungnir is said to have been made by the dwarfs—Ívaldi's sons.

á Grana brjósti. Völsunga Saga reads *gygjar brjósti.* Grani was Sigurðr's horse.

This list may be compared with the objects found in the Maglehøi tomb. Cp. p. 42 above and S. Müller, *Nord. Alt.* I. p. 354.

18. *hverfðar við inn helga mjöð. Völs. Saga* reads—*hræðar* or *hræðar* (? *hrærðar*). Perhaps explained by reference to *Sigrdr.* 5 or *Guðrúnarkviða* II. 22. Egilsson and others cp. *Háv.* 144 f.

af skafnar...rístnar. Cp. *Skírnismál* 36 : *svá ek þat af ríst sem ek þat á reist.*

19. For *bjargrúnar, ölrúnar,* cp. str. 9 and 7.

bókrúnar, lit. 'runes inscribed on beech rods.' Cp. *bók-stafr.* According to Egilsson the reference is to inscribed chips of wood placed in the horn.

meginrúnar, presumably runes of (magical) strength.

óviltar. Cp. *Atlamál* 9.

20. *hvassa vápna hlynr,* a kenning, lit. 'maple of sharp swords.'

21. This strophe is spoken by Sigurðr.

The following strophes are given in a prose paraphrase in *Völsunga S.* XXI (Sigrdrífa is now again the speaker): *ver vel við frændr þína ok hefn lítt mótgerða við þá ok ber við þol ok tekr þú þar við langæligt lof.*

22. Cp. *Völs. S.*

23. *símar,* lit. 'threads,' presumably of Fate; cp. *Helg. Hund.* I. 3. Most editors emend to *limar* by analogy with *Reginsmál* 4. Cp. also Þjóðolfr Arnórsson, 4, 10. In these cases *limar* seems to mean 'consequences.' Cp. *Völsunga S.* prose version : *grimm hefnd fylgir griðrofi.* For the sentiment expressed, cp. *Völuspá* 39.

vára vargr. Várar is generally used with reference to marriage. This may possibly be a reference to Sigurðr's subsequent history in connection with Brynhildr.

24. This precept is found also in the *Loddfáfnismál* and would seem to be stock advice.

25. The *Völsunga S.* prose paraphrase reads : *verð lítt mishugi við óvitra menn á fjölmennum mötum : þeir mæla opt verra en þeir viti, ok ertu þegar bleyðimaðr kallaðr ok ætlaðr, at þú sér sönnu sagðr ; drep hann annars dags ok gjalt hánum svá heiptyrði.*

27. *hvars skolo reiðir vega.* Cp. *Fáfnismál* 17, *reiðir* for *vreiðir.* Cp. *Háv.* 32, note.

The phrase corresponding to *bölvísar konor* in the *Völsunga S.* is *vandar vættir.*

28. R reads *sifja silfr,* i.e. 'the silver of relationship by marriage' (cp. *Sigurðarkviða in skamma* 15); Bugge emends to *sifjar silfrs,* i.e. 'Sifs of silver,' a kenning for 'ladies.' Cp. the sentiment expressed in *Háv.* 115 etc. The *Völsunga S.* prose paraphrase reads : *Lát eigi tæla þik fagrar konur, þótt þú sjáir at veizlum, svá at þat standi þér fyrir svefni eða þú fáir af því hugarekka, teyg þær ekki at þér með kossum eða annarri blíðu.*

konor, perhaps 'married woman.'

31. Both in the *Gulaþingslög*, p. 46 and in the *Grágás* LXXXVI the penalties for burning a man in his house are enumerated. Such an offender was called *brennu vargr*.

37. *at vinom.* Cp. *Völs. S.*

In *Völs. S.* at this point the betrothal of Sigurðr and Sigrdrífa takes place.

THE REGINSMÁL

Sigurðr on his way to attack the sons of Hundingr receives on board his ship Hnikarr, who in the *þáttr af Nornagesti* is called *heklumaðr* (i.e. the man wearing a hood), but who is really Óðinn in disguise. Str. 19 is spoken by Sigurðr, the following strophes by Hnikarr.

19. *at sverða svipon,* a kenning for battle. Cp. our phrase 'shock of arms.' **R** omits the direction *Sigurðr kvað*; the *þáttr af Nornagesti* has *Sigurðr kvað til heklumanns.*

20. In a fragment from the *Málskrúðsfrœði* (Gering, p. 476) we find :

> *Flugo hrafnar tveir   af Hnikars öxlum*
> *Huginn til hanga   en á hræ Muninn.*

Throughout the Edda there are frequent references to Óðinn's ravens ; cp. also the story of Haakon the Bad, *Saga of Ólaf Tryggvason*, XXVIII (Heimskr.); *Landnámabók*, ii, XXXIII.

21. *á tái.* F. Jónsson compares Old Danish *fodta* (*Arkiv*, XIV. 267 ff.), and would translate, 'stone elevation in front of a house.' Cp. also *Guðrúnarhvöt* 9.

22. *þá.* If this refers to *úlfr* the change from sing. to pl. is awkward. Gering translates 'if you see them (your opponents) before (they see you)'—*fyrri* being adv. in this case.

23. A rational piece of advice.

systur Mána. Cp. *Vafþrúðnismál* 23, 'Mundilfari is the name of the father of Máni and also of Sól.'

hamalt fylkja. There are frequent descriptions of this type of battle formation in Norse literature. In the story of the battle of Brávellir, it is attributed to Óðinn, Saxo, p. 317 ; *Skjöldunga Saga*, Brot., cap. 8. This strophe is in the *fornyrðislag* metre.

24. *Dísir.* Cp. *Hamðismál* 28, in which the murder of Erpr is attributed to the Dísir, *hvöttumk at dísir.* The Dísir are frequently referred to in Norse literature as supernatural beings. In the Edda they are generally associated with war and death. *Grímnismál* 53 seems to be based on the same idea as that expressed here. In *Njáls S.* XCVI we are told that Þíðrandi was slain by the Dísir. Cp. Brand, *Popular Antiquities*, II. p. 570.

25. Wilken, *Pros. Edda*, Glossar. s.v. *fyrir.* For other interpretations see Vigfusson, Egilsson, Gering (s.v. *heill, fyr*).

For similar advice, cp. *Háv.* 61 and the description in *Wallingford's Chronicle* (Gale, p. 547).

Is the significance of this strophe that men may come to *Valhöll* in the evening, i.e. die a sudden death ?

THE GRÓGALDR

The dead Gróa is awakened by her son Svipdagr who asks her for spells to ensure his safety and success in his quest for the maiden Menglöð.

5. *verða allr.* Cp. the similar phrase in the late poem *Íslendingadrápa* 9. The lit. meaning seems to be 'complete,' 'brought to an end.' *afi,* i.e. 'man' (cp. *Skírnismál* 1). The more usual meaning is 'grandfather,' cp. *Vafþrúðnismál* 29. A wise woman called Gróa is mentioned in the *Skaldskaparmál* XVII.

6. *fjölnýtan.* Cp. *Sigrdr.* 4.
Rindr Rani, so the MSS read. Most editors adopt Vigfusson's emendation *Rindi Rani* and explain the allusion by Saxo, p. 128, where Óðinn bewitches Rinda, the daughter of the Ruthenian king, *cortice carminibus adnotato contingens,* and by *Hrólfs S. Kraka* XXXIX, where Óðinn gives himself the name Hrani ; cp. also *seið Yggr til Rindar,* *Skaldskaparmál* LIV. The difficulty of the MS reading, however, may be accounted for by a reference to a lost story. In the *Gylfaginning* XXX, XXXVI, Rindr is the name of the mother of Vali.
sjálfr...þik. Cp. *Hugsvinnsmál* 29, 6, *sjálfr kenn þú sjálfan þik.*

7. *árna* (cp. Gothic *airinōn*), a rare word, probably explained by str. 3.
Urðar lokkor. Cp. *Háv.* 111, *Völuspá* 19, and the *varðlokkur* (*Thorfinns S. Karlsefnis* III).
smán. In prose the word means 'shame, disgrace.' Many editors emend here, with Bugge, to *á sinnom sér.*

8. *þjóðáar.* If we adopt this emendation we may compare the names of rivers enumerated in the *Grímnismál* 27-29. Horn and Ruðr are not included in the list nor do they occur elsewhere ; but cp. Bugge's note.
fjörlotom. ἅπ. λεγ. Cp. the compound *líflát* ; Bugge emends to *fjörlokum* by analogy with *aldr-lok.*
snúiz til heljar meðan. Most editors emend to *heðan* by analogy with the same phrase in *Grímnismál* 28, *Fáfnismál* 35 and 40.

9. *galgvegi.* This reading would seem to be a reference to *Fjölsvinnsmál* 45, where Menglöð threatens Svipdagr with hanging:

> Horskir hrafnar   skulo þér á hám gálga
> slíta sjónir ór.

If however the rendering *gaglvegi* is the original, then we might compare *gagl-viðr* (*Völuspá* 42).

10. *leysigaldr.* So Bugge emends, by analogy with Bede, *Hist. Eccl.* IV. 22, *alysendlican.* This emendation agrees in sense with the verb *kveðinn* unless this verb is used with meaning *kvaddr* ('invoked'). The MSS readings are obscure ; *Leifnir* is the name of a sea king in *Þulur* IV. a, 4, and is used in kennings for sea and for gold (cf. *Leifnis laut, Leifnis grund*) ; there is also a giant called Leifi (*ib.* b, 5).

11. *meira,* perhaps 'more stormy,' 'violent.' Cp. Egilsson s.v. and Detter and Heinzel, *ad loc.*
logn ok lögr. Many editors emend with Grundtvig to *lopt ok lögr* and would translate 'wind and wave.' Is the MS reading *logn ok lögr* a hendiadys ? or does *lögr* stand for the runic symbol ?
luðr. So the MSS read. Bugge emends to *lið* and the passage would then seem to mean : 'may wind and wave conspire to help you.' The

use of *lúðr* here should be compared with the use of the word in the *Fjölsvinnsmál* 30, which may very well have some bearing on this passage—as well as in *Vafþrúðnismál* 35. The meaning has not been satisfactorily cleared up in any of these passages. The word may contain an allusion to a lost mythological episode. Fritzner, however, compares *veðrbelgr* and its use in *Þorsteins Saga Víkingssonar* XI : *ek á einn belg þann er veðrbelgr heitir, en ef ek hristi hann þá stendr úr honum stormr ok vindr*; one could then perhaps compare *Odyssey* X. 19 ff.

12. *hrævakulði*. Cp. Falk, *Arkiv*, IX. pp. 347, 356.
haldiz æ lík. Cp. Egilsson, s.v. *halda* C, 2.

13. *at því...megit*. Cp. Egilsson, s.v. *fjarri*.
kristin dauð kona. Does this point to an early date ? Detter and Heinzel suggest that the phrase would be impossible in the eleventh century.

14. *naddgöfga*. Cp. *Hyndluljóð* 35.
gnóga. ἁπ. λεγ. Most editors take adverbially. Egilsson considers this unlikely and suggests that *gnóga* is a mistake for *gnótt* or *gnægð*.
The reading *minni ok hjarta* is suggested by Detter and Heinzel as the probable reading of the MS. The phrase is quoted by Vigfusson as occurring in *Passíu-Sálmar*; Bugge however emends to *munn ok hjarta*, an emendation adopted by many editors. He suggests that the abbreviation for *ok* used in the MS might well be confused with *z* (whence *s*).

CPSIA information can be obtained at www.ICGtesting.com
Printed in the USA
239182LV00001B/3/P

9 781107 679764